SRI LA

also available in the **Series on Religion, Nationalism, and Intolerance**

# SRI LANKA

## THE INVENTION OF
# ENMITY

### DAVID LITTLE

Series on
Religion, Nationalism, and Intolerance

UNITED STATES INSTITUTE OF PEACE PRESS
Washington, D.C.

The views expressed in this book are those of the authors alone. They do not necessarily reflect views of the United States Institute of Peace.

United States Institute of Peace
1550 M Street, N.W.
Washington, D.C. 20005-1708

First published 1994

Printed in the United States of America

The text of this book is set in Palatino; the display type is Futura. Cover design by Ana Eastep and Day W. Dosch; interior design by Joan Englehardt and Day W. Dosch. Page makeup by Helene Y. Redmond of HYR Graphics.

The paper used in this publication meets the minimum requirements of the American National Standard for Information Sciences—Permanence of Paper for Printed Library Materials, ANSI Z39.48-1984.

**Library of Congress Cataloging-in-Publication Data**
Little, David, 1933–
    Sri Lanka : the invention of enmity / David Little.
        p.  cm. — (Series on religion, nationalism, and intolerance)
    "Based on a conference entitled 'Religious Intolerance and Conflict in Sri Lanka'"
    Includes index.
    ISBN 1-878379-15-1 (alk. paper)
    1. Sri Lanka—Politics and government.  2. Sri Lanka—Ethnic relations.  3. Tamil (Indic people)—Sri Lanka—Politics and government.  4. Buddhism and politics—Sri Lanka.  I. Title.  II. Series.
DS489.8.L58  1993
954.9303—dc20                                                    94-1061
                                                                      CIP

Nationalism is not what it seems, and above all not what it seems to itself. The cultures it claims to defend and revive are often its own inventions. . . .
—Ernest Gellner, *Nations and Nationalism*

Nationalism is an invented political community, yet to describe it as "invented" . . . is to link it not to "falsity" and "fabrication" but to "imagination" and "creation". . . . I do not believe there was "nationalism" as such in Sri Lanka a thousand years before the rise of the nation-state in the New World and Europe, but something . . . was there, ready to be transformed.
—Steven Kemper, *The Presence of the Past*

# Contents

# Foreword

In the Cold War years, conflict among various religious communities was characteristically viewed through the prism of the East-West struggle. Few analysts of international affairs foresaw that with the dramatic changes in Eastern Europe, the former Soviet Union, and elsewhere, religion would come to occupy an increasingly prominent place in questions of war and peace, and violence driven by religious belief would require more rather than less attention as a source of international conflict.

The Series on Religion, Nationalism, and Intolerance is one of the ways that the United States Institute of Peace is focusing on this challenging topic. The first volume in the series, *Ukraine: The Legacy of Intolerance* (1991), and the Sri Lanka study, taken together make a strong case for giving careful consideration to the role of religion in ethnic tensions and related international conflicts.

There is no suggestion in either study that religion alone is the cause of tension. Conflict, whether of the milder sort evident in Ukraine, or of the more violent kind in Sri Lanka, is normally a complicated affair. It is not necessary to believe that religion explains everything in order to appreciate the importance of religion in contemporary international conflicts.

The two case studies make clear that the nationalist impulse—the aspiration of an ethnic group to achieve political control over a given territory—often must search for legitimacy, which religion sometimes provides. Nationalists want their cause to have the broadest possible justification and popular support, and religious traditions are an important means to achieving both.

In the independence movement against Russian control, the Ukrainian Catholic and the Ukrainian Orthodox churches supplied some sacred reference points around which nationalists rallied. At the same time, the long-standing tensions over jurisdiction and the restoration of church property between the Ukrainian and Russian Orthodox, and occasionally between the Orthodox and the Catholics, have been a continuing cause of antagonism within Ukraine.

In Sri Lanka, Buddhist revivalism was the result of many factors. It was a reaction to colonialism, to a deep sense of cultural isolation and insecurity, and to the modern imperatives of nation-building. As such, it sought to recover and restore to preeminence what revivalists took to be the ancient prerogative of the Sinhala majority, and especially of its language and religion. The influence of some Buddhist monks in the revivalist movement underscores the salience of religion. Tamil revivalists, responding in part to Sinhala assertiveness, employed appeals similar in form to those of their Sinhala counterparts by demanding a political arrangement favorable to protecting their ethnic identity and interests.

In short, the ongoing conflict between the Sinhala and the Tamils that has ebbed and flowed for close to half a century derives its emotional force, in part, from competing and mutually exclusive beliefs about legitimate rule and sacred authority.

By implication, both cases also demonstrate the relevance to conflict amelioration of the values of tolerance, pluralism, and nondiscrimination—norms that are enshrined in documents such as the UN Declaration against Intolerance. This conclusion is of special interest because such norms establish the terms of reference for the Institute's entire Series on Religion, Nationalism, and Intolerance, of which the books on Ukraine and Sri Lanka are a part.

Despite the driving force of religious commitment in both these communities, the idea of creating a genuinely multiethnic and multireligious national identity has significant support in both countries. In Ukraine, the Popular Front in Support of Perestroika (Rukh) is an influential group that continues to advocate such views. In Sri Lanka many of the conditions of ethnic cooperation, such as lingual equality, increased minority autonomy within a federal system, and respect for ethnic diversity, enjoy substantial public acceptance today. Of course, there remain daunting obstacles to the realization of tolerance and pluralism in both societies, but there is also reason for hope and opportunity for amelioration of tensions.

The Series on Religion, Nationalism, and Intolerance is a project of the Institute Working Group on Religion, Ideology, and Peace, which was established to consider how religions and similar belief systems contribute to conflict situations, as well as to discover methods for managing such conflicts and encouraging reconciliation and toleration of communal differences.

As the basis for this publication series, the working group is conducting six two-day conferences over a period of four years. The group has already considered Ukraine, Sri Lanka, Lebanon, Sudan and Nigeria (together), and Tibet, and it will take up Israel in 1994. The cases have been chosen to assess differing cultural and belief traditions, various geographical and political settings, and diverse types of intolerance. Some of the cases—particularly Sri Lanka, Lebanon, Sudan, Nigeria, and Israel—are of special interest because at one time or another these societies have been committed to the principles of religious tolerance and pluralism. All the cases illustrate the ways in which the modern imperatives of nationalism set the context for much of the religious and ideological conflict that is becoming a major characteristic of our times. By focusing on these important examples, the working group hopes to draw useful conclusions about the causes of this type of conflict as well as prospects for its amelioration or peaceful management.

Richard H. Solomon, President
United States Institute of Peace

# Preface

In keeping with the series of which it is a part, this volume approaches ethnic conflict in Sri Lanka with an eye to the special role of religion and religious intolerance.

Since the salience of religion may not be taken for granted, the book tries to sort out and trace just where and how the "religious factor" plays into the tensions between the Sinhala majority and the Tamil minority that have dominated life in Sri Lanka since the 1950s. It attempts to show that the struggle by Sri Lankans to define for themselves an appropriate national identity after independence from the British in 1948 is incomprehensible apart from the religious identities embraced by the two groups—predominantly Theravada Buddhism for the Sinhala and Saivite Hinduism for the Tamils.

The book is particularly attentive to the special circumstances surrounding the conjunction of religion and what emerge as conflicting and incompatible images of nationhood held by the two communities. The volume tries to show, accordingly, that the term "religious intolerance," if carefully understood and precisely applied, illuminates important aspects of the conflict.

The relevant "special circumstances" turn out, in part at least, to be of relatively recent origin. The colonial experience, especially in connection with the British during the nineteenth century, and the growing pressures of nationalism in the nineteenth and twentieth centuries, provided the indispensable context for "the invention of enmity." At the same time, the peculiar dynamics of that context prompted each party to turn back to its own ancient spiritual heritage, and to revive and adapt that heritage in helping to define its image of nationhood. In that respect, the sources of intolerance in Sri Lanka are a complex mixture of the modern and the ancient.

Laying bare the roots of intolerance requires, therefore, some attention to history, and in that regard, this study is a chronicle of the rise and manifestation of intolerance in Sri Lanka. But the results of the study also suggest a useful direction for overcoming intolerance, and in that way can perhaps contribute to a reduction of enmity in Sri Lanka.

The book is divided into two parts. The first part, "Belief and Intolerance," analyses the sources of "revivalism" in Sri Lanka, both for the Sinhala and for the Tamils. Here religious belief is shown to provide justification for certain forms of cultural and linguistic ethnocentrism. The second part, "Patterns of Conflict," recounts the record of the stormy relations between the Sinhala and the Tamils from roughly the 1920s to the present. An attempt is made throughout to connect the analysis with the broader concerns of the general study that are outlined in the section "About the Series."

This book is based on a conference entitled "Religious Intolerance and Conflict in Sri Lanka" that took place at the United States Institute of Peace on September 4 and 5, 1990.

The conference was organized around four major paper presenters. Sarath Amunugama, fellow at the International Center for Ethnic Studies in Colombo, Sri Lanka, presented a paper entitled "Buddhaputra and Bhumiputra? Dilemmas of Modern Sinhala Buddhist Monks in Relation to Ethnic and Political Conflict." Amunugama has published widely on Sri Lankan society and literature, including several books.

Patrick Peebles, professor in the Department of History at the University of Missouri, Kansas City, delivered a paper entitled "The Accelerated Mahaweli Programme and Ethnic Conflict." Peebles was a visiting professor in history at the

University of Peradeniya in Sri Lanka in 1984, and visiting associate professor of South Asian history at Cornell University in 1988–89.

John Rogers, research fellow at the Center of South Asian and Indian Ocean Studies at Tufts University, presented a paper entitled "Regionalism and Ethnicity in Sri Lanka." Rogers is the author of *Crime, Justice and Society in Colonial Sri Lanka*.

H. L. Seneviratne, associate professor of anthropology at the University of Virginia, presented a paper entitled "South Indian Cultural Nationalism and Separatism in Sri Lanka." Seneviratne has conducted anthropological field work in Sri Lanka, specializing in the sociology of Buddhism. He is author of *Rituals of the Kandyan State*.

Four respondents also participated. Stanley Tambiah is a professor of anthropology at Harvard University and the author of several books, including *Sri Lanka: Ethnic Fratricide and the Dismantling of Democracy* and *World Conqueror and World Renouncer*, a study of Buddhism in Thailand. C. R. de Silva, associate professor and lecturer at the University of Peradeniya, Sri Lanka, is currently chair of the Department of History at Indiana State University. In addition to being the author of over ten books and over forty articles, de Silva edited *The American Impact on Sri Lanka*. George Bond, professor of history and religion at Northwestern University, has written extensively on Buddhism in Sri Lanka and was the recipient of a Fulbright grant for research in Sri Lanka. He is author of *The Buddhist Revival in Sri Lanka: Religious Tradition, Reinterpretation, and Response*. Sarath Perinbanayagam, professor of sociology at the City University of New York, Hunter College, has written several books on Sri Lanka, including *The Karmic Theater: Self-Society and Astrology in Jaffna*.

The author gratefully acknowledges the contributions of all those who participated in the original conference. Without their help—as well as that of the members of the Working Group on Religion, Ideology, and Peace, the conference speakers and respondents, and the many individuals, especially in Sri Lanka, who have provided such invaluable information and instruction—the preparation of this volume would have been impossible.

In particular, H. L. Seneviratne's contribution was immeasurable. He helped plan the original conference on Sri Lanka; he has been a limitless source of background material and suggestions based on his own current work on the Buddhist monks of Sri Lanka; he has read and reread drafts of the manuscript, always giving pointed and incisive reaction; and he has spent hours helping to clarify and recast central ideas in this report. In addition, several of the conference participants offered invaluable advice on the manuscript: John Rogers, Stanley Tambiah, George Bond, C. R. de Silva, Sarath Perinbanayagam, and Vernon Mendis. Sarath Amunugama was his usual generous and affable self in acting as host for a trip the author took to Sri Lanka in the summer of 1991. Besides that, Amunugama made the results of his current research available and offered illuminating counsel regarding the themes of this book. Finally, he arranged interviews with numerous political figures, journalists, and religious leaders, together with several people whose views and reactions, both oral and written, have been very influential on this study: Neelan Tiruchelvam, Radhika Coomaraswamy, Reggie Siriwardene, K. M. de Silva, and S. W. R. de A. Samarasinghe. Special gratitude is due de Silva and Samarasinghe for lengthy and illuminating discussions, both in Sri Lanka and in Washington, D.C., as well as for the readiness with which each of them made available a number of recent writings on Sri Lanka. Both men, too, have offered very helpful comments on the manuscript.

Certain members of the working group went out of their way to make useful suggestions, especially John Kelsay, Rosalind Hackett, Ian Lustick, and Ann Elizabeth Mayer; many of those suggestions have been duly incorporated. Marion Creekmore, former U.S. ambassador to Sri Lanka, very kindly read the manuscript, and shared some very helpful observations and reactions.

Timothy Sisk, former program assistant, played an indispensable role by helping to plan and conduct the conference and then by transcribing the proceedings. Scott Hibbard, the present program assistant, has performed invaluable service by aiding in the preparation of the manuscript. Special thanks also to Dan Snodderly, editorial manager at the Institute, for his graceful goading and expert assistance.

Nonetheless, the author bears the full and final responsibility for the views expressed in this volume. The views do not represent the position of the United States Institute of Peace or, necessarily, that of any of the people associated with the conference, or of those who have been consulted in the course of preparing this document. In a subject as sensitive as this one, involving many diverse and often conflicting interpretations, it is impossible to harmonize all opinions and suggestions. Judgments and selections must be made, and therefore some people who have so generously assisted the author will not be fully satisfied. That is both regrettable and inevitable. But whatever the remaining flaws in this study, it is much the stronger for having been subjected to such diverse, thoughtful, and challenging review.

# About the Series

This six-part study of belief and intolerance considers how and why certain religious and similar beliefs create or contribute to hostility and conflict, as well as how and why they are frequently a cause of discrimination and persecution. In addition, it addresses the prospects and techniques for modifying and ameliorating conflicts that involve religious and similar loyalties and commitments. It asks how stable arrangements of mutual respect and forbearance come about. What are the resources, both inside and outside traditions of belief, that encourage "peaceful pluralism" and thereby prevent differences in basic outlook from leading to mistreatment, abuse, and violence?

Such an investigation is squarely within the mandate of the United States Institute of Peace. The Institute is an independent, nonpartisan government institution created and funded by Congress to strengthen the nation's capacity to promote the peaceful resolution of international conflict (or conflict with serious international implications). The Institute pursues its mandate by awarding grants, by appointing scholars and practitioners as fellows, by producing publications and educational programs, and by assembling working groups to share ideas and conduct research.

The study is the project of the Institute Working Group on Religion, Ideology, and Peace. By directing the attention of twenty-five or so experts to the subject of belief and intolerance, we expect to draw some useful conclusions regarding one aspect, at least, of the causes of serious conflict and the means of resolving it.

The context for this reflection will be six two-day conferences spread over a period of roughly four years. Each conference is devoted to an area of the world where serious intercommunal tension or conflict exists and where intolerance based on religion or belief appears to be a significant part of the difficulty. The working group has already taken up Ukraine, Sri Lanka, Lebanon, Sudan and Nigeria (in combination), and Tibet; it will consider Israel in 1994. Reports on these conferences, written by the director of the working group, David Little, will follow in due course.

The inspiration for the study is the momentous set of concerns enunciated in the UN Declaration on the Elimination of All Forms of Intolerance and of Discrimination Based on Religion or Belief, adopted by the UN General Assembly in November 1981. In view of the fact, states the preamble, "that the disregard and infringement of human rights and fundamental freedoms of thought, conscience, religion or whatever belief, have brought . . . wars and great suffering to mankind," the General Assembly declares itself to be "convinced that freedom of religion and belief should . . . contribute to the attainment of the goals of world peace, social justice and friendship among peoples. . . . "

Widespread violation of religious liberty and freedom of conscience make such a study urgent. According to information compiled by the UN special rapporteur on intolerance and discrimination, "infringement of the rights defined in the Declaration against Intolerance seem to persist in most regions of the world. . . . They concern all the provisions of the Declaration."[1]

> The Special Rapporteur is concerned with the persistence of alarming infringements of other human rights arising out of attacks on freedom of thought, conscience, religion or belief. Noteworthy among them is the growing number of extra-judicial killings that have allegedly taken place in the context of clashes between religious groups or between such groups and security forces. Resorting to violence or the threat of its use in dealing

with problems or antagonisms of a religious nature is also a disturbing development which, if unchecked, might endanger international peace.[2]

The most important factors hampering the implementation of the Declaration are: the existence of legal provisions that run counter to the spirit and letter of the Declaration; practices by governmental authorities; contradicting not only the principles embodied in international instruments but even provisions enshrined in domestic law which prohibit discrimination on religious grounds; the persistence of political, economic and cultural factors which result from complex historical processes and which are at the basis of current expressions of religious intolerance [p. 56].

In some instances, a state's constitution extends special privileges by conferring official status on one religious or ideological group. In others, special legislation favors one or more religions to the detriment of excluded groups, and in extreme examples, certain religions or denominations are declared to be unlawful and members are punished for belonging to those groups or practicing their tenets (p. 11).

Beyond legislative provisions, government practices and policies frequently violate the terms of the declaration by encouraging disparagement of specific groups by means of the state-controlled media, educational policy, or denying in practice any legal status or legal protection to the members of a religion not recognized officially. Governments sometimes tolerate and even encourage abuses perpetrated by one group against another, or directly interfere in the practices and activities of certain religious bodies (pp. 11–12).

Finally, political, economic, and cultural factors frequently breed distrust and bigotry.

Norms, judgments, prejudices, superstitions, myths, and archetypes whereby we model our behavior in society and which are culturally transmitted from generation to generation, as well as anachronistic and unjust economic structures that result in regional majorities of human beings sunk into misery and ignorance, all foster the germination of dogmatism, intolerance, and discrimination, and with it persecution and armed aggression. These norms, judgments and prejudices, which give rise to deep feelings and to the transformation of unfocused emotions into sharp feelings that condition our ideas about equality among human beings, as well as tolerance and respect for the ideas and feelings of others, are a product of societal forces. This means that in order to eliminate discrimination and intolerance in all its forms there must necessarily be a change in attitude of the human being which will be a product of the needed social changes and psychic transformations of individuals.[3]

The declaration is clear that *all* forms of basic belief, and not just religious belief, are explicitly protected. People may not be punished or discriminated against, regardless of whether their basic beliefs are religious.[4]

However, the declaration is not altogether clear or consistent about the exact meaning of intolerance.[5] At one point, intolerance is synonymous, and used interchangeably, with discrimination (see Appendix, article 2.2). To discriminate, according to the declaration, is to impose a restriction or preference "based on religion or belief" that denies basic human rights and freedoms, such as freedom of expression, freedom of worship, equal access to public facilities, and so on. It is presumed, incidentally, that the declaration also prohibits persecution, or the direct infliction of severe injury or distress, as simply an extreme form of discrimination.

At another point, however, the declaration suggests that intolerance and discrimination are different things. The title itself speaks of "the Elimination of All Forms of Intolerance *and* of Discrimination" (emphasis added). What is more, states are obligated under the declaration to prohibit discrimination legislatively, but they are urged "to take all appropriate measures to combat intolerance" (see Appendix, article 4.2), as though they were dealing with distinct phenomena.

Perhaps the proper interpretation is that, strictly speaking, intolerance refers to motives and attitudes, whereas discrimination refers to acts. Accordingly, "intolerance describes the emotional, psychological, philosophical and religious attitudes that may prompt acts of discrimination. . . . "[6] This formulation raises the related question whether the outward expression of intolerant attitudes—such as taunting, insulting, or inflaming people because of belief—while not constituting actual discrimination as such, is still prohibited under the declaration insofar as it may be shown to incite discrimination. Such a proposition, of course, poses standard perplexities concerning the proper limits of free speech.[7]

Bearing the proposed distinction between intolerance and discrimination in mind, it will, in this study, nevertheless be convenient (and not altogether inconsistent with the declaration or with ordinary usage) to use the word *intolerance* occasionally in a less refined and more inclusive way to cover acts of discrimination (and persecution) as well as motives and attitudes that incite to such action. In that sense, *intolerance based on religion or belief* may at times refer to abusive practices as well as to the feelings and dispositions behind those practices.[8]

It is important to emphasize the specific and rather elaborate sense in which the word *intolerance* is used in the declaration to counteract the lingering suspicion that the very notions of tolerance and intolerance are outmoded and need to be replaced. The word *tolerance* recalls, it is said, arrangements in which a majority merely indulges certain unconventional beliefs as a matter of sufferance, not of right. On that basis, adherents are hardly given equal respect or treated without discrimination. According to this older notion, those unwilling to bear with such an indulgent system would be called intolerant. But under contemporary conditions, the idea of intolerance appears to convey considerably more than that.[9]

However accurate this observation may be historically, the concept of intolerance as specified in the declaration prohibits all arrangements that rest on or produce attitudes or conditions of serious discrimination or the demeaning of certain groups because of religion or belief. By implication, the idea of tolerance would exclude any such attitudes and conditions.

A central objective of the project, then, is to test carefully and thoughtfully the twofold proposition that intolerance, as described, contributes substantially to wars and great suffering and that its modification or elimination helps to promote justice, solidarity, and peace.

## Approach

The comparative study of intolerance and belief, such as is described here, has not been taken up elsewhere. It represents, it is hoped, a distinctive complement to related work in regard to nation-building, communal conflict, and human rights.

The study is not envisioned as a rigorous social-scientific exercise replete with quantified results aimed at verifying some comprehensive theory of intolerance. The subject matter is so complex and varies so from place to place that it appears at this stage to defy any such aspiration. A more exploratory, informal, and open-ended approach seems preferable.

Moreover, whatever explanatory account is finally adopted for why people believe as they do and what they make of their beliefs, there is no substitute for first determining carefully what those beliefs are and how believers themselves understand, defend, apply, and are disposed to alter their beliefs. Unless that job is done well, explanatory accounts will be deficient. In short, the study takes seriously the subjective meaning of belief as expressed by participants and informed observers of the areas to be examined.

It should also be said that—for working purposes, at least— a *belief* shall be understood as a state of mind disposed to regard a proposition or set of propositions as true. *Belief that* something is true seems to be a necessary condition for holding a belief, however expanded the idea may become when people talk, as they often do in discussions of religious and ideological matters, of *believing in* someone or something. The kind of special trust, confidence, or commitment usually associated with basic or fundamental beliefs of a religious or related sort seems to presuppose that those beliefs are taken to be true in the first place.[10]

This emphasis on belief does not mean that the investigation is indifferent to material factors, such as the motive to protect or achieve sheer economic or political advantage for one's group. These factors are sometimes understood to be external to the core doctrines of the respective belief traditions and to condition in various ways the connections between belief and intolerance. Part of the task of the study will be to detect and trace those connections, at least informally and suggestively, insofar as they exist.

Such a task is, of course, notoriously complicated, because basic religious and other beliefs so readily become entangled with questions of ethnic, economic, and national identity and competition. On the one hand, religious or other basic beliefs are occasionally manipulated in the service of political or economic interests. Machiavelli's famous advice to princes comes to mind:

> It is well to seem merciful, faithful, humane, sincere, religious, and also to be so; but you must have the mind so disposed that when it is needful to be otherwise you may be able to change to the opposite qualities. . . . A prince must take great care that nothing goes out his mouth which is not full of the above . . . qualities, and, to see and hear him, he should seem to be all mercy, faith, integrity, humanity, and religion. . . . [N]othing is more necessary than to seem to have this last quality. . . . Everybody sees what you appear to be, few feel what you are. . . . A certain prince . . . never does anything but preach peace and good faith, but he is really a great enemy to both, and either of them, had he observed them, would have lost him state or reputation on many occasions.[11]

On the other hand, religion or similar beliefs typically play an active and prominent part in defining group identity and in picking out and legitimating particular ethnic and national objectives. For example, political and economic competition among groups is frequently couched in religious terms, and attitudes toward members of other groups and ways of treating them are themselves understood religiously.

Max Weber reminds us of "the need of social strata, privileged through existing political, social, and economic orders, to have their social and economic positions 'legitimized.'" Groups "wish to see their positions transformed from purely factual power relations into a cosmos of acquired rights, and to know that [those rights] are thus sanctified."[12] The fact that human beings seem compelled to evaluate given political and economic arrangements in reference to sacred or cosmic standards suggests that religious and related beliefs play a special role in human experience and are more than simply the function of some prior material or external condition.

If religion and like beliefs were but the function of something else, it remains to be explained why conflicts over political legitimacy so readily and so recurringly get expressed in religious and similarly ultimate categories, and why those categories continue to have such wide and vital appeal. Why, exactly, does the struggle for dominance in so many places—in Sudan, Sri Lanka, Tibet, Ukraine, Israel—have such a conspicuous and enduring religious dimension?

These considerations support the importance of attending explicitly to religious and similar beliefs in a study of intolerance while not losing sight of whatever conditioning circumstances are found to be relevant. This sort of orientation seems important in respect to understanding not just the sources of intolerance, but also the means for modifying or eliminating them.

One way of refining this kind of investigation is to develop a typology of possible relations between belief and intolerance that accommodates and helps to clarify the complexity of subject matter that has already been alluded to. The following is a preliminary attempt.

The general distinction between belief as a *target of* intolerance and belief as a *warrant for* intolerance is suggested by what have been called the twin principles of the UN Declaration against Intolerance: the principle of "the freedom to manifest religion or belief, stated in Article 1," and the principle of "the freedom from discrimination based on religion or belief, set forth in Article 2."[13]

The first principle is designed to protect people from becoming targets of intolerance—that is, from being disadvantaged, confined, or injured for holding and expressing certain beliefs and for performing certain practices. While the way beliefs and practices are perceived varies according to circumstance, three general categories of belief as a target of intolerance may be enumerated: the unorthodox, the politicized, and the seditious.

The first category, *unorthodox belief,* refers to a religious or ideological belief perceived as intolerable from the point of view of the orthodox belief system. The second category, *politicized belief,* refers to a religious or ideological belief perceived as threatening the existing polity simply by virtue of recommending an alternative government structure or character. *Seditious belief,* finally, refers to a religious or ideological belief perceived as constituting incitement to active rebellion against an existing government.[14]

The second principle of the UN Declaration against Intolerance is designed to prevent people from using religion as a warrant for perpetrating acts of intolerance—that is, disadvantaging, confining, or injuring others in the name of a certain religion or belief. Belief as a warrant for intolerance refers to a belief held by a dominant group that is taken to entitle that group to act intolerantly toward others.

It should be emphasized that the two kinds of intolerance are not necessarily correlative. There could be nonreligious grounds for discriminating against a religious sect, as, for example, when a secular state harasses a group of Jehovah's Witnesses who refuse to offer unqualified devotion to the government. Similarly, there could be religious reasons for discriminating against a group that itself is identified not by religion but rather by race, language, or some other nonreligious indicator. An example would be treating African-Americans or women unequally on the basis of a scriptural text or theological doctrine.

## Primary Concerns of the Study

Sensitive to these categories and distinctions, this study has been conceived in light of three primary concerns:

1. To identify the character and degree of intolerance in each respective setting: Is belief the target of discrimination or

persecution or both? What sort of belief is targeted (unorthodox, politicized, seditious)? What form does discrimination or persecution take? Is belief a warrant for discrimination or persecution? What form does discrimination or persecution take?

2. To identify and analyse the justifications (religious or non-religious) for intolerant treatment, as well as the responses of those subject to such treatment. (Here the various connections among belief and political legitimacy, ethnic identity, and national identity would be relevant.)

3. To determine the degree to which existing beliefs (and their justifications) may be treated more tolerantly if they are the target of intolerance and may become more tolerant or "pluralistic" if they are a warrant for intolerance.

The foregoing comments about giving beliefs their due without ignoring conditioning circumstances would be particularly pertinent at points 2 and 3.

# PART I:

# BELIEF AND INTOLERANCE

# SRI LANKA

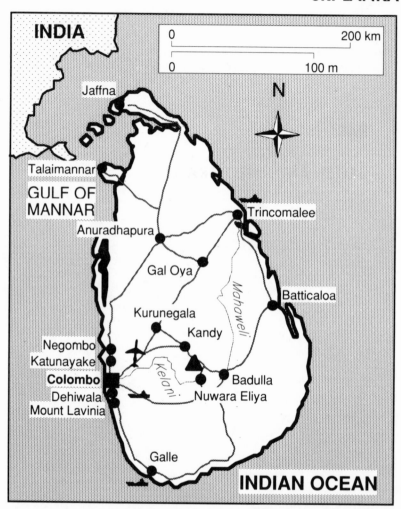

From *Maps on File.* ©1989 by Martin Greenwald Associates. Reprinted with permission of Facts on File Inc., New York.

*one*

# Introduction

"It cannot be repeated too often that the present tragic situation is the product of specific historical circumstances, and not, as one often hears in Sri Lanka and in the international press, the end product of a 2,500-year-old struggle between ancient enemies."[1]

The "present tragic situation" began to emerge only in the early twentieth century. It consists most importantly of recurrent violence and severe tension between the majority Sinhala population (75 percent), predominantly Buddhist, and the Tamil minority (18 percent), mainly Hindu, with a few Christians in both groups. More precisely, the conflict has most directly involved the indigenous "Sri Lankan Tamils" (12 percent), as distinct from the "Estate" or "Indian Tamils" (6 percent), whom the British started importing in the nineteenth century to work on the tea and coffee plantations. There is also a small population of Muslims (7 percent), who mostly speak Tamil but distinguish themselves by their religion and in fact continue to experience their own tension with parts of the Tamil community.

Ideas of exclusive communal identity and of hostile competition over questions of race, language, ethnicity, religion, and political control took shape between the Sinhala and the Tamils in the period leading up to 1948, when Ceylon, as it was then known, gained its independence from the British. Thereafter, some of the ideas were put into practice.

3

Conditions at the time of independence need not have encouraged intercommunal intolerance. The Tamil community was fairly small. Even though Indian Tamils were not satisfied with their lot, and some Sri Lankan Tamils had begun worrying about their future, Tamil interests might, under some circumstances, have been satisfied relatively easily. Moreover, many Tamils had lived in Sri Lanka from antiquity, frequently intermingling with the Sinhala majority and developing long-standing patterns of mutual accommodation and tolerance.

Unlike India's experience at the end of colonial rule, which included severe religious and ethnic animosity between Hindu and Muslim, Sri Lanka's transition to independence was comparatively calm. As the British departed, both Tamils and Sinhala were left in positions of authority. That was partly because the colonial educational system had produced an intercommunal elite with a shared language and common values and partly because, by training, the members of the elite had learned the art of political adjustment and compromise within the framework of a fledgling constitutional democracy.[2]

But appearance did not coincide with reality. Shortly after independence, there commenced a pattern of chronic intercommunal violence and hostility that has not yet been eliminated. The first major outbreak occurred in May 1958. The newly elected prime minister, S. W. R. D. Bandaranaike, and the Sri Lanka Freedom Party (SLFP) he led, achieved power in 1956, with the strong support of Buddhist leaders, by campaigning for the primacy of Sinhala language, culture, and religion. The Tamils took offense. Inspired by Gandhi's campaigns of civil disobedience against the British in India, they mounted a series of *satyagraha* (civil disobedience) demonstrations to protest the new policies, only to provoke violent retaliation by the Sinhala.

In 1971 there was an outburst of violence that initially concerned only the Sinhala but that eventually had dire consequences for the Tamils. Economic failure caused severe unemployment, which particularly affected the youth of the land. In response, Sinhala young people connected to a vaguely Maoist revolutionary organization called Janatha Vimukthi Peramuna (JVP) assaulted police stations in parts of the island. Worsening economic conditions only exacerbated the plight of Tamil youth, who as the result of government policies had begun to find it more difficult than before to gain admission to programs in professional education and to find employment in the public sector.[3]

In addition, the new constitution of 1972, drafted and adopted in the face of strong Tamil dissent, appeared to the Tamils to be a product of majority dictatorship and the cultural chauvinism of the Sinhala.[4] Although all other faiths were given equal protection, Buddhism was accorded "the foremost place," and the state was directed "to protect and foster" it. Equally contentious was the constitutional provision making Sinhala the official language, with the use of Tamil permissible by statute. For the first time various groups of Tamils united against Sinhala dominance, and Tamil leaders began to talk openly of secession.

The next instance of major violence, in August 1977, was also associated, like the outbreak in 1958, with a divisive national election. J. R. Jayewardene of the United National Party (UNP) displaced the SLFP in a landslide victory, paving the way for what the Tamils saw as further consolidation of Sinhala power at their expense. Though Tamils had strongly supported the Jayewardene ticket, and its promise of improved ethnic relations, they were soon disappointed. An incident in Jaffna "precipitated a ferocious outbreak of communal violence between the Sinhalese and Tamils . . . which spread to many parts of the island and bore comparison with the ethnic disturbances of the mid-1950s."[5] For the first time, Tamil youth, in retaliation, took up violence against the Sinhala.

With a substantial mandate from the majority and part of the minority, Jayewardene undertook to reorder and reshape national policy and to support new procedures for controlling the violence, which appeared to be increasing. Along with liberalizing the economy, he favored a Gaullist constitution, adopted in 1978, which centralized power in the hands of the president. Although the constitution retained some features objectionable to the Tamils, such as still ascribing "the foremost place" to Buddhism, it did include certain concessions to the Tamils. It upgraded the status of the Tamil language and instituted proportional representation for parliament and direct election of the president, which appeared to provide more equitable representation. New government policies assured the Tamils easier access to university admission and allocated power at the local level in the form of district development councils. Finally, there was some hope that a more liberal, free-market economy might give Tamils a greater chance for economic improvement.[6]

However, several factors worked to counteract these concessions, preventing improved relations between the two groups. The government, internally divided over treatment of the Tamils, lacked resolve in implementing the new directives. The district development councils failed to become effective agencies of local control, mainly through lack of financial support. Finally, "Buddhism enjoyed a growing measure of expressive hegemony in the Jayewardene years," reinforcing the preeminence of Sinhala identity.[7]

Disillusioned and frustrated with what they regarded as halfway measures, and encouraged by the Indian government in Delhi and Madras, as well as by Tamil expatriates living in Tamil Nadu and in the West, some Tamil groups turned to violence, which, in turn, increased apprehension in the Sinhala community. In response, and in hopes of heading off civil war, the Jayewardene administration imposed stringent emergency measures, such as the Prevention of Terrorism Act of 1979. This act became the basis for an aggressive and highly controversial campaign against the Tamils in the northern province.

Growing tensions between the Sinhala and the Tamils caused some sporadic outbursts of violence in 1981, and then erupted, devastatingly, in the riots of July 1983. These riots, principally centered in Colombo and the suburbs, exhibited unprecedented ferocity and destructiveness. Hundreds of

Tamils were killed, and thousands more lost their property and became refugees as the result of rampaging Sinhala crowds who were indulged and here and there incited by security forces.

The government's response to these distressing developments, including imposing more controversial emergency measures, only intensified polarization and enmity between the two communities. Things were further complicated by India's growing interest and involvement in the Sri Lankan conflict. Loyalty and common identity had long existed between South Indian and Sri Lankan Tamils, and that connection began at the time to yield tangible support for the Tamil cause in Sri Lanka. But more than that, the Indira Gandhi government saw political advantage in providing support. The prospect of more than a hundred thousand refugees fleeing to India to escape the violence of 1983 reenforced Mrs. Gandhi's commitment to train and finance Sri Lankan Tamil guerrillas, as well as to help arrange a settlement that would, in her eyes, protect Tamil interests in Sri Lanka.[8]

The Liberation Tigers of Tamil Eelam (LTTE) were the major beneficiaries of Indian intervention. Fighting for nothing less than a separate state, they raised the level of violence against government forces and Sinhala civilians, and eventually drove the Sri Lankan army out of the Jaffna peninsula in the north. But when, in 1987, the army attempted to regain control of the area, the Indian government objected, forestalling Sri Lankan efforts. India then succeeded in pressuring the Jayewardene administration, despite strenuous Sri Lankan popular resistance, into accepting the Indo–Sri Lankan Agreement to Establish Peace and Normalcy in Sri Lanka, signed by Rajiv Gandhi and J. R. Jayewardene on July 29, 1987.

The agreement established the basis for a multiethnic, multilingual plural society, in which all citizens might live "in equality, safety and harmony." Tamil and English were identified alongside Sinhala as official languages. Administrative power was to be devolved to the temporarily unified northern and eastern provinces, which contained the majority of Tamils, leaving the final connection between the two provinces to be worked out later. In addition, the agreement imposed a ceasefire, called for the Tamil guerrillas to be disarmed, and authorized an Indian peacekeeping force (IPKF) to implement the arrangement.

Initial reactions were positive. Tamil reception was at first enthusiastic, and for a while the government succeeded in subduing Sinhala opposition to the agreement that was staged especially by the JVP and the Movement for Protecting the Motherland (Mavbima Surakime Vyaparaya).[9]

However, the agreement soon collapsed, and was replaced, once again, by violence. The JVP could not long be contained, and they mounted a campaign of terror against those who sympathized with the agreement. For their part, the LTTE, who had not been included in the negotiations, took up arms against the Sri Lankan government and the IPKF, as well as against those among the Tamils who sympathized with the agreement.

As the situation worsened, Jayewardene's prime minister, Ranasinghe Premadasa, was elected president of Sri Lanka in December 1988. In reponse to growing Sinhala resentment toward the Indo–Sri Lankan Agreement, Premadasa initiated talks with the LTTE, who were at the time weakened by their struggle against the IPKF. This interval enabled the Sri Lankan government to devote itself to an intensive campaign against the JVP. Aided in this endeavor by pro-government death squads, Premadasa succeeded in subduing the JVP by the end of 1989.

In addition, Premadasa negotiated the withdrawal of the IPKF, who were suffering unanticipated losses, and were beginning to lose interest in the whole operation. By March 1990, they were gone, though not before inadvertently strengthening the LTTE and thereby worsening the conflict. The Tamil National Army left behind by the Indians immediately collapsed, and with almost no effort the LTTE improved their position by taking possession of huge stocks of sophisticated weapons and supplies.

Thereafter, the conflict settled down into a relatively localized, if still expensive and bloody, civil war between the

LTTE and the Sri Lankan army in the northern and eastern provinces. In late 1992 there was a flurry of interest in working out a new peace accord by expanding the terms of the Indo–Sri Lankan Agreement. By early 1993 there was some indication that government military gains had provided an incentive for seeking new talks with the LTTE. The LTTE, too, hinted they might be willing to compromise.

However, the prospects for resolving the ethnic conflict in Sri Lanka have been obscured by the sudden assassination of President Premadasa on May Day, 1993, apparently as a consequence of an LTTE plot. Initial fears of Sinhala retaliation against the Tamils have not materialized, and the new president, D. B. Wijetunge, has professed willingness to enter into talks with the LTTE. But to date, the civil war and the growing number of casualties persist.

*two*

# The Colonial Background of Sinhala Identity

## The Missionary Factor

The bitter, sometimes violent, intercommunal strife between the Sinhala and the Tamils did not materialize until the twentieth century. Although some of the antecedents of this strife were ancient,[1] most are to be found in the nineteenth century, during the British colonial period.[2]

### The Portuguese and the Dutch

No doubt the colonial predecessors of the British—the Portuguese (1505–68) and the Dutch (1568–1796)—encouraged one kind of religious intolerance. They made certain groups the target of mistreatment and discrimination because of their religious orientation.[3]

Whether it was the aggressive Catholicism of the one or the militant Calvinism of the other, both powers left behind a record of religious oppression. Buddhists, Hindus, and Muslims all suffered under Portuguese persecution. The Dutch were a bit less zealous, sometimes employing economic and civil rewards as inducements to conversion.[4] For political reasons, the Dutch tolerated the Buddhists while making things hard for the other groups and, as might be

expected, they added Roman Catholic converts to their enemies list.[5]

Antagonism certainly existed among the peoples of Sri
Lanka before the arrival of colonialism and Christianity, but
until then there was no general pattern of intolerance among
different religious groups.[6] From time to time, Buddhist rulers had used force to suppress certain forms of heterodoxy,
but such action applied only to the *sangha* or monastic community.[7] The suppression did not affect the population at
large. Ordinary members of society were not singled out and
targeted for disparagement or mistreatment because of their
religious beliefs or affiliations. Allegiance to a particular ruler
or regime did not carry with it an expectation of religious
conformity, as it did for the Portuguese and the Dutch.[8]
"Ethnic, religious, and linguistic differences were not used
[in premodern Sri Lanka] as the bases for inclusion or exclusion from the polity. At various times, groups would
speak alternative languages, adhere to alternative religions,
and claim alternative identities."[9] In that sense, it is "quite
correct to say that the first experience of religious intolerance
comes with the Christian missions."[10]

### The British

During their period of colonial rule (1796–1948), the British
played a distinctive role in the "full scale ideological attack
on Hinduism, Buddhism and local folk traditions"[11] that was
perpetrated under colonialism. At first, it was the Christian
missionaries, not the colonial government, that led the way.[12]
The Anglicans and the Methodists, having established themselves in the early part of the nineteenth century, were in the
forefront pursuing their own brand of aggressive evangelism
through preaching, education, and pamphleteering.[13]

Some of the missionaries learned the language well enough
but insisted on using forms of address that to indigenous
ears sounded highly insulting. They undertook to acquaint
themselves with the beliefs and customs of the Sri Lankans,
but primarily to be "the better prepared to expose their

absurdity and sinfulness."[14] Between 1849 and 1861 alone, mission presses produced an estimated one-and-a-half million polemical tracts in Sinhala and English. The publications were regarded as an effective means of assaulting "this wretched system," "this stronghold of Satan."[15]

But the missionaries' most successful weapon was education. The British established a new system of government- and church-run schools, displacing traditional Buddhist education and thereby stripping the monks of one of their primary functions in Sinhala society.[16] A curriculum regarded as "worse than useless," as consisting of nothing but the study of a few sacred books, astrology, and "the superstitious and speculative mystical philosophies of the East,"[17] was replaced by the study of Christianity and western science and humanities. The objective was to gradually elevate the natives to a more advanced social level by exposing them to the benefits of western civilization—benefits taken to be infinitely superior to anything Buddhist culture might offer. The effect was to reduce to some extent awareness of the Buddhist and Sinhala heritage.

The British colonial government gradually turned to assisting the missionaries in their struggle against Sinhala Buddhism,[18] as the example of education makes clear. Government policies transformed education and gave special privileges and advantages to the missionaries in administering many of the schools,[19] even though the different Christian groups struggled among themselves over what they regarded as their fair share of government support. Similarly, the government came to cooperate with the missionaries in defining the more general relations between religion and the state.

In 1815, the British extended and solidified their rule over the island by negotiating control of the Kandyan region in central Sri Lanka. In exchange for this control, the British accepted the Kandyan Convention, agreeing to respect "the religion of the Boodhoo professed by the chiefs and inhabitants of these provinces" and to maintain and protect "its rites, ministers, and places of worship."[20] From the beginning, the government showed in at least two ways that it was not as

wholehearted about encouraging and supporting Buddhism as
the Kandyan elite expected. First, the government's general
attitude of neutrality in religious affairs was quite alien.
According to Sinhala tradition, it was not enough for the
government simply to refrain from interfering in religion
and to provide some legal protection, as the British were doing.
The government needed to take a more active role. Monastic
officials had to be appointed, stipends granted, sacred objects
cared for, and monastic rights over "temporalities" (certain
forms of property and wealth) enforced. In addition, the
effects of the policies of various British officials over the
years did not seem all that neutral to the Sinhala anyway.
"The picture of the Christians as a privileged group, and of
the Anglican church as the church of the elite persisted, even
after the disestablishment of the Anglican church in 1881."[21]

The missionaries encouraged the government not only to
continue to ignore its obligations implied in the Kandyan
Convention but in fact to sever all connection with Buddhism.
From their point of view, the Kandyan Convention was
misbegotten to begin with; it amounted to nothing more than
the indulgence of "heathenism." As a result of vigorous
missionary opposition, including the publication in 1839 of
an influential pamphlet, *The British Government and the Idolatry
of Ceylon*,[22] the British gradually withdrew their support and
by the middle of the nineteenth century had adopted legislation renouncing "all active participation in practices at once
idolatrous and immoral."[23]

> In no aspect of policy did the impact of evangelicalism loom
> larger than on the question of the severance of the connection
> of the state with Buddhism. Indeed, the increasing influence of
> evangelicalism brought with it an inevitable hardening of relig-
> ious attitudes, a positive assertion of the superiority of Christi-
> anity over other religions, and a general contempt for Oriental
> religions and cultures.[24]

Severing the connection between Buddhism and the state
became an important source of resentment in the Buddhist
community, resentment that caused continuing agitation

throughout the late nineteenth century for a more sympathetic British policy.[25] By the 1870s, the British turned pragmatic and worked out a more accommodating attitude toward the Buddhists, though they would still not go far enough to suit the extremists.[26]

## Racial Theories

Beliefs about racial superiority, which gained prominence in the late nineteenth and early twentieth centuries in the West, undergirded the attitudes of the colonial government and the missionaries and eventually had a profound, if complex, effect on the self-understanding of the Sri Lankan people.[27] The basic premise of these beliefs was that race—particularly as linked to language—is the primary determinant of social identity and of a civilization's worth. Since certain races self-evidently qualify as "chosen people," they have a special warrant to dominate and acculturate others. To the British, one of the unmistakable sources of colonial authority was the obvious superiority of Anglo-Saxon culture, language, and religion. These straightforward chauvinistic convictions reinforced missionary efforts to subdue Sri Lankan culture.

At the same time, there were other equally important implications of racial thinking that, ironically, had partially contradictory effects. Inspired by the burgeoning field of comparative historical and linguistic studies, British and other European observers invoked racial categories to analyze Sri Lankan society. Books began appearing in the mid-nineteenth century arguing that the peoples of Sri Lanka were naturally divided along racial-linguistic lines.

One author contended that "the proper inhabitants of the island," the Sinhala Buddhists, had over centuries been forced to defend themselves against invaders from southern India, who were of a very different racial-linguistic stock.[28] The invaders were supposed to have degraded what had been a remarkable Sinhala civilization, comparable to ancient Greece and Rome. Benighted peoples like the Portuguese and the Dutch only hastened the decline. To be sure, the British, as the representatives of a sublime civilization, were now compelled to come to the rescue of the Sinhala so that they might overcome the infirmities imposed by others and might progress to a new level of cultural achievement.[29] Views of this kind naturally sowed the seeds of ethnic division and resentment.

In the late nineteenth century, ethnic analysis became more explicit and more assertive, particularly as a theory about the nature and origins of the "Aryan race" attracted increasing attention. According to the theory, certain structural affinities between Indian and European languages were thought to be rooted in common racial attributes characteristic of "Aryans." Aryans were supposedly a non-Semitic Caucasian people with a common language, who were eventually dispersed throughout various parts of Asia and Europe. On the basis of intricate philological studies, proponents argued that Sinhala, derived as it is from Sanskrit, is actually an Indo-European language. Therefore, by hypothesis, the Sinhala people, along with the North Indians from whom they were believed to be descended, counted as Aryans.

This line of reasoning had some portentous implications. British and other western advocates of the Aryan theory had, wittingly or not, provided the Sinhala "with a prestigious 'pedigree,'"[30] which could be used to good advantage in competition with other Sri Lankan groups, such as the Tamils. If, unlike the Tamils, for example, the Sinhala were racially related to their colonial masters, did they not, after all, share in the masters' superiority of race and consequent right to rule others? Of course, looked at another way, that same implication could double back and work against the British. If the Sinhala and the British shared the same racially based prerogatives, the reasons for continued colonial dominance were also called into question. Such were the ironies of racism.

But whatever the complexities, the primary belief in British superiority won out in the end. Anglicized Sinhala adapted to colonial ways and culture, only to find that "the British would never allow them to become full partners in their society. . . . They had acquired the British viewpoint but were allowed neither to mix socially with the British nor to assume top leadership positions in business and government."[31] "The cant of Exeter Hall—'we are brethren'—has no influence out of England."[32] This treatment would not be forgotten.

## The Search for Identity: The Sinhala Buddhist Response

In the early stages, Buddhist leadership was generally forbearing in the face of missionary treatment and governmental policies built on ideas of British superiority. There was, it is true, some mild protest in the 1820s. Petitions emphasized the distress the missionary campaign caused the Buddhists, and it was suggested that the government preserve a policy of religious tolerance by prohibiting offensive publications and public statements.[33] In general, however, the monks were accommodating. They assisted the missionaries with translations, permitted use of public halls, lent copies of Buddhist scriptures, and gave itinerants a place to stay. This response, however, only intensified the hostility of the missionaries. Gestures of generosity were taken as signs of "indolence, apathy, and indifference in all matters of religion." One missionary remarked that "there is often an appearance about [their faces] of great vacancy, amounting almost to imbecility."[34]

But by the latter half of the nineteenth century, these attitudes began to change appreciably. One missionary returning to Sri Lanka in the 1860s "was delighted to note that the pernicious vice of tolerance was on the wane."[35] Monks were no longer so eager to cooperate with the missionaries but, on the contrary, initiated a counteroffensive of their own. Borrowing tactics from their opponents, they formed groups such as the Society for the Propagation of Buddhism, and they purchased printing presses to disseminate their teachings.[36]

Although the monks had earlier avoided challenges to debate the missionaries, in the 1860s and 1870s they finally agreed. They participated in a series of written and oral exchanges in which they answered the charges so long leveled against them and attempted to refute claims that Christianity is superior to Buddhism. Of one such encounter in 1864 a missionary reported that "never before in Ceylon was there such a marshalling of the enemy against Christianity. The one aim of the fifty priests and their two thousand followers . . . was not to defend Buddhism but to over-throw Christianity."[37]

Perhaps the most famous debate took place in 1873 at Panadura, a town south of Colombo, where a well-known monk, Mohottivatte Gunananda, faced off against a Methodist leader, David de Silva. The event took two days, and by the second day, ten thousand people, mostly highly partisan Buddhists, were in attendance. Ironically, an important part of Gunananda's counterattack on Christianity was drawn from western antireligious arguments. The boisterous and widely heralded public verdict was that Gunananda triumphed over his Christian opponents; Buddhism had been vindicated.[38]

With this debate, the cultural tide turned decisively.[39] Gunananda's victory symbolized the beginning of the Bud-dhist revival in Sri Lanka, which would gather strength during the rest of the nineteenth and into the twentieth century. Part of the revival was the revitalization and reac-tivation of Sinhala-educated monks and lay people, though some members of the British-educated urban elites were also attracted. Part of it, too, was the emergence of Buddhist newpapers that mobilized sentiment in favor of Buddhist education, confrontation with the missionaries, construction of temples, and so on. But most of all, the Buddhist revival supplied the basis for a new Sinhala identity reconstructed in opposition to the identity fostered by the missionaries and the colonial administration.[40]

Several things stand out about the new Sinhala identity. It was to an important extent formed in reaction to coloni-alism, and its religious component—namely, Buddhism—was essential.[41] In a word, it was "religion that first provided a framework for [the] Sinhala to challenge the ideological domi-nance of colonialism."[42] Moreover, this new identity bore with it all the marks of "incipient nationalism," and as such it represented a long-term threat to the political culture nur-tured by the British.[43]

*three*

# Sinhala Buddhist Revivalism

## "New Corn from Old Fields"

The Buddhist revival of the late nineteenth century deviated in important ways from traditional Buddhism. As a consequence of colonial, and especially British, influence, the revival mirrored many key religious and cultural patterns introduced from the outside, and it cannot be understood apart from modern influences. At the same time, the Buddhist revival was not a "totally new invention . . . which could have been given almost any content."[1] However reconstituted, however reshaped, something deep within the tradition was after all "revived." There is both continuity and discontinuity with the past.

On the one hand, the revivalists undoubtedly did absorb certain elements of missionary religion. Whether the result amounted to a kind of "Protestant Buddhism," as has been claimed, is a controversial matter.[2] There is little question that the form of Buddhism adopted by the emerging Sinhala urban middle class displayed some "Protestant" features, such as an emphasis on lay responsibility that was generally absent from the tradition.[3] Such change was, of course, partly a matter of necessity. As mentioned, the sangha was demoralized and fragmented in many places because of the lack of British support and because of educational and other reforms. But another reason was that the Buddhist revivalists

19

modeled themselves after their colonial rulers, becoming, in
some respects, "missionar[ies] writ large."[4]

In addition, there was a new attachment to "scriptural
Buddhism which would have been inconceivable in the times
of Sinhala Kings,"[5] a disposition in part reminiscent of the
Biblicism of the missionaries. Revivalists typically "turned
to the texts to find authoritative foundations for their rein-
terpretations. The lack of . . . strong Buddhist leadership or
institutional presence in the late colonial period made this
move especially necessary as a basis for reform."[6]

Beyond that, the new Buddhist leaders adopted many of
the traits and objectives of the missionaries. They affected
the same aggressive oratorical style. They disparaged "alleged
non-Buddhist ritual practices and magical manipulations"[7]
in favor of economic industriousness, social and political
reform, and other kinds of "this-worldly activity." They also
shared the conviction, dear to the hearts of nineteenth-
century British Protestants, that religion is a central and
inextricable part of cultural and political life—a vital index,
so to speak, of national and racial identity.

On the other hand, Buddhist revivalists, unlike typical
Protestants, did not altogether reject monasticism, magic, or
ritualism. Even though the monks and the monasteries took
on a distinctly "this-worldly" tone, one decidedly oriented
toward social and political change, the *bhikkhus*, as the monks
were known, would continue to play an important and sometimes decisive role in Sri Lankan life, precisely because of
their position as monks.

In fact, revivalist Buddhism appears in some respects and
for certain groups to have become increasingly "monas-
ticized." Observance of certain regular religious days, for
example, implied "a kind of temporary monasticism for the
laity"; newly founded meditation centers were "modelled on
the routines of monastic forest hermitages," and there was
"an ever-increasing presence of monks at various [funeral
and marriage] rites."[8]

Accordingly, Sinhala Buddhism "remain[ed], on the whole,
an extremely ritually oriented religious tradition, especially

in terms of its public ethos."[9] Ritualized religious celebrations of family, community, and national events continued to be numerous and frequent. Moreover, the passion of the Sinhala in modern times to erect public images of the Buddha does not reflect a particularly Protestant attitude, as Protestantism characteristically opposes the display of religious images.[10]

In short, while there can be no doubt that colonialism in general and English Protestantism in particular were indispensable in stimulating and shaping the emergence of Buddhist revivalism, it seems unlikely that those influences were all that mattered. Certain features of Buddhist revivalism bear an unmistakably indigenous stamp.

### Anagarika Dharmapala

A leading exemplar and formative figure was Anagarika Dharmapala, "the homeless guardian of the Dharma," as he called himself. His stormy career and fiery rhetoric dedicated to the cause of Buddhist revivalism symbolize the combined effects of indigenous and colonial influences on the movement.[11]

Don David Hewavitarne, as he was originally known, was born in 1864, the son of a successful businessman and active lay Buddhist. Significantly, Hewavitarne received much of his formal education in Christian schools, though he continued to study Buddhism and local languages on the side.[12] He was frequently subjected to evangelistic appeals, and he invested considerable time and energy in mastering Christian scripture and in acquainting himself with missionary educational techniques.

Hewavitarne's parents encouraged him to attend to his Buddhist heritage, and they placed him under the care of some of the most influential monks of the period. One was Mohottivatte Gunananda, who had successfully stood up to the Christians in the famous Panadura debate of 1873. In fact, Hewavitarne was present at that debate and described Gunananda as "a golden tongued orator, winning in personality.... [W]hen he began replying to Christian attacks on Buddhism, his fame soon spread over the island."[13] And

Hewavitarne goes on to draw an unflattering comparison between monks like Gunananda and the missionaries: "In contrast to my wine-drinking, meat-eating and pleasure-loving missionary teachers, the bhikkhus were meek and abstemious. I loved their company and would sit quietly in a corner and listen to their wise discourse, even when it was far above my head."[14]

Interestingly enough, Gunananda's influence on Hewavitarne was itself shaped by the West. Gunananda was acquainted with and sympathetic to the Theosophical Society, founded in America in 1875 by Madame Helena Blavatsky and Colonel Henry Steele Olcott, a former Union officer in the American Civil War. Theosophy advanced a belief in universal mysticism strongly oriented toward Buddhism and Hinduism. Gunananda had corresponded with Blavatsky and Olcott, and translated part of a book by Madame Blavatsky into Sinhala. When the leaders of the Theosophical Society visited Colombo in 1880, Gunananda saw to it that his sixteen-year-old charge was present for their public lectures, and that he became acquainted with them.

The purpose of the visit was to strengthen the Buddhist cause against the missionaries. Olcott and Blavatsky had got wind of the Panadura debate in a New York publication, and detected an opportunity to help Buddhism reassert itself in Asia. But before that could happen, Buddhism would need to reform and modernize itself in several ways. To defeat the missionaries, it would be necessary to distill and make readily accessible the essentials of Buddhism, being particularly careful to disentangle them from the vulgar and superstitious accretions that had over the years distorted the true message. Buddhists also needed to establish schools to propagate their teachings, and they needed to start building cooperation among fellow Buddhists throughout Asia.

Beginning with the visit in 1880, Theosophical "influence on Sri Lankan Buddhism was both immediate and long lasting."[15] The immediate impact was indeed remarkable, as Olcott reports: "The Sinhala people *en masse* gave us a princely reception. . . . Triumphal arches; flags flying in every town, village and hamlet; roads lined with *olla* fringes for miles together; monster audiences gathered together to hear and see us—these evidences of exuberant joy and warm affection astounded us."[16] Capitalizing on this enthusiastic reception, Olcott quickly published *The Buddhist Catechism*, which claimed to capture the essence of Buddhism in popular form and thereby provide a rallying point for mobilizing and unifying the Sinhala. Soon thereafter he founded the Buddhist Theosophical Society (BTS), and by 1898 he had established a hundred or so BTS schools. The schools mostly mimicked the missionary model, and many of them became highly successful in disseminating "the basic religious ideology of the educated Buddhist bourgeoisie."[17]

Very soon this kind of agitation increased tensions between Buddhists and Christians. The Buddhists, filled with new energy and a sense of purpose, began asserting themselves, and on Easter Sunday, 1883, a large procession celebrating the completion of a new addition to Gunananda's temple in Colombo was attacked by Catholics as it passed Saint Lucia's Cathedral. One person was killed and thirty injured.

The event galvanized the Buddhists. It also had a decisive impact on Dharmapala. In protest against the attack, Dharmapala's father immediately removed his son from the Catholic school he was attending, and the young man began meeting regularly with local officials of the Theosophical Society, soon becoming a member by special arrangement. The intense association with Colonel Olcott and Madame Blavatsky that followed was of lasting importance, even though Dharmapala would eventually turn his back on Theosophy.

Olcott and Blavatsky encouraged Dharmapala to learn Pali, the language of classical Buddhism, and to immerse himself in the study of Buddhist doctrine. Under their influence, he eventually resolved to live a celibate life and to take up his homeless identity. He journeyed with Olcott and Blavatsky to India and consequently embraced the cause of restoring Buddhist holy places there, something that would consume considerable time and energy throughout the rest of his life.

While the Theosophical movement initially stimulated and
deepened Dharmapala's commitment to Buddhism, he found
it, finally, insufficiently dedicated to the cause of Buddhism,
and he rejected the movement in 1904.[18] Its strong ties to
Hinduism were particularly galling to Dharmapala because
of his efforts to liberate Buddhist shrines in India from what
he regarded as illicit Hindu domination.

Two years later Dharmapala founded his influential newspaper, *Sinhala Bauddhaya* (Sinhala Buddhist), probably the
first appearance of the term.[19] Together with his associate,
Piyadasa Sirisena, eminent novelist and editor of *Sinhala
Bauddhaya*, he thereby began an energetic career devoted to
Buddhist revivalism and Sinhala nationalism.[20] Though he
had little immediate impact on the political elite of his day,[21]
he provided the vision and laid the intellectual foundations
for a movement that would eventually have the greatest
consequence for Sri Lanka. In the long run, Dharmapala
"was undoubtedly the most influential individual in the Buddhist revival in Sri Lanka";[22] as such he came to serve as "a
model for . . . Buddhist activists."[23]

### *"Sons of Buddha, Sons of the Soil"*[24]

Dharmapala laid out the major themes of his message in 1902:

> This bright, beautiful island was made into a paradise by the
> Aryan Sinhala before its destruction was brought about by the
> barbaric vandals. . . . Christianity and polytheism are responsi-
> ble for the vulgar practices of killing animals, prostitution,
> licentiousness, lying and drunkenness. . . . This ancient, historic,
> refined people, under the diabolism of vicious paganism, intro-
> duced by the British administrators, are now declining and
> slowly dying away. The bureaucratic administrators . . . have
> cut down primeval forests to plant tea; have introduced opium,
> ganja, whisky, arrack and other alcoholic poisons; have killed
> all industries and made the people indolent.[25]

The passage exemplifies the anticolonialist assumption that
the Sinhala are a chosen people, a people of special worth,
"ancient, historic, refined," entitled and therefore uniquely

able to administer "this bright, beautiful island" as it was destined to be administered. Conversely, the frustration and corruption of that preordained mission is the result of alien intervention by "barbaric vandals," by those racially, culturally, and morally inferior to the Sinhala—particularly, though not exclusively, the British. What more could be expected from people like the British, uncivilized as they were until comparatively recently, than "vulgar practices" and injurious policies?

But perhaps most important of all is the underlying idea that the successful governance of Sri Lanka is at bottom about religion. If "the diabolism of vicious paganism" and "Christianity and polytheism" are responsible for the moral and physical evisceration of Sri Lanka, then only by substituting correct religion can Sri Lanka prosper:

> Under the influence of [Buddha's] religion of righteousness, the people flourished. Kings spent all their wealth in building temples, public baths, [pagodas], libraries, monasteries, rest houses, . . . schools, . . . waterworks and beautified the city of Anuradhapura, whose fame reached Egypt, Greece, Rome, China, India and other countries.[26]

In short, Dharmapala's reasons for rejecting British imperialism were not political or economic. They were religious: above all, the Sinhala nation is the historical custodian of Buddhism. "Imperialism had to be resisted since it threatened the survival and integrity of the traditional Sinhala way of life which had preserved the Buddha's teaching."[27]

In continually emphasizing the historical warrants for the mission entrusted to the Sinhala, Dharmapala exhibits what has been called the Sinhala "obsession with the ancient past."[28] He insisted that there must be a reawakening of commitment "for the preservation of our nation, our literature, our land and our most glorious religion at whose source our forefathers drank for nearly seventy generations."[29] "Let the methods adopted in the ancient days by the good kings of old, like [Duttagamani], Buddhadasa, Parakrama Bahu, and other rulers be adopted."[30] Duttagamani was particularly worthy of note. Dharmapala heralded this warrior king of the

second century B.C. as "a rallying figure for Sinhala youths."[31]
He had heroically "rescued Buddhism and our nationalism"[32] by liberating Sri Lanka from the foreign domination
of Tamil rulers.

But for Dharmapala the sources of the sacred Sinhala
legacy extended well back before the second century B.C.

> Two thousand four hundred and forty six years ago a colony
> of Aryans from the city of Sinhapura in Bengal . . . sailed . . . in
> search of fresh pastures. The descendants of the Aryan colonists
> were called Sinhala after their city, Sinhapura, which was
> founded by Sinhababu, the lion-armed king. The lion-armed
> descendants are the present Sinhala, whose ancestors had never
> been conquered, and in whose veins no savage blood is found.
> Ethnologically, the Sinhala are a unique race, inasmuch as they
> can boast that they have no slave blood in them, and never were
> conquered by either the pagan Tamils or European vandals
> who for three centuries devastated the land, destroyed ancient
> temples, burnt valuable libraries, and nearly annihilated the
> historic race.[33]

## The Use and Abuse of History

Dharmapala's observations on Sri Lankan history are drawn
from the ancient Pali chronicles of the island, known as the
*Dipavamsa* (Island Chronicle), the *Mahavamsa* (Great Chronicle), and the *Culavamsa* (Little Chronicle).[34] Though these
documents record among them critical political events over
some two thousand years of Sri Lankan history, focusing
particularly on the exploits and fortunes of notable kings,
they are not so much a simple dynastic genealogy—let alone
a general history—as an account of Buddhism in Sri Lanka.[35]
More specifically, they constitute "the sacred history of a
people destined with a sacred mission, namely, to maintain
the purity of the Dhamma in a world of impermanence and
self-seeking."[36]

Consequently, the chronicles have a mythical aspect. Historical facts are embellished in various ways to lay the foundations for the "charter" of an ideal social order.[37] Though

Dharmapala and the other Buddhist revivalists clearly reconstructed the charter implicit in the chronicles for their own
purposes, certain basic features of it would resonate power-
fully in a time of incipient nationalism during the late colonial
and postcolonial periods.[38]

The heart of the charter implied in the chronicles and the
part that appealed particularly to Dharmapala is "the unity
of nation and religion"[39] and, more precisely, the inseparable
connection between state and sangha. The chronicles are
history written by and from the perspective of Theravada
Buddhist monks,[40] and the original purpose of the chronicles
"was to celebrate the relationship between the Theravada
monkhood . . . and the monarchy."[41] In supporting the
sangha, the king is understood, above all, to be the defender
of the faith. Only if the Theravada sangha have their material
needs provided for by the king, and are duly protected
against heresy, disputes, and corruption can prosperity and
tranquillity thrive in the land.

Significantly, the sacred history recorded in the chronicles
begins with a decision by the Buddha himself to visit the
island and to make it "a fit dwelling place for men,"[42] where
"his doctrine should (thereafter) shine in glory."[43] He accom-
plishes that goal by banishing the original inhabitants of the
island, disruptive and malevolent groups of subhumans known
as the Yakkhas and the Nagas. Buddha thereby makes room
for Vijaya, an immigrant from North India, who becomes
the founding hero and first king of Sri Lanka. Born of a
union between a lion and a human, Vijaya determines the
identity of his descendants as Sinhala, or "people of the
lion," and he cements the connection between them and
Buddhism. "Vijaya . . . is come to Lanka," where "my religion
[will be] established,"[44] as Buddha is said to have put it.

According to the earliest chronicle, the *Dipavamsa*, Buddha
takes pity on the plight of the expelled Yakkhas and Nagas.
He proceeds to provide an appealing home for them elsewhere, displacing them more by inducement than by terror.
Through his benevolence, Buddha elevates the image of
the nonviolent and compassionate ruler. By contrast, the

*Mahavamsa*, which was of special interest to Dharmapala, sets a much more violent precedent.[45] In that account, Buddha makes no provision for the well-being of the Yakkhas and the Nagas but summarily frightens them off with ominous supernatural acts. The image of the ideal Buddhist ruler is, accordingly, considerably more ferocious than in the *Dipavamsa* and is best exemplified by Dharmapala's favorite warrior king, Duttagamani, or "Ghamini, the enraged," as he is known.

The *Mahavamsa* devotes extensive attention to Duttagamani. By creating what has been called "the Duttagamani epic," it establishes him as "the paradigm of the righteous Buddhist king" and thus as the premier member of the "cult of heroes" believed to be central to the Sinhala tradition.[46] The account begins with Duttagamani's decision to relinquish his status as a pious monk and to be born the son of a Buddhist queen, "endowed with all auspicious signs"[47] befitting a future king. At a young age, he is outraged over the subjugation of the Buddhists to a non-Buddhist king. He lies contorted on his bed, symbolizing his inability to stretch out because of the Tamils on the one side and the ocean on the other. Resolving to set things right, Duttagamani proceeds to eliminate thirty or so potentates throughout Sri Lanka and eventually restores Buddhist dominance "under one parasol of state" by subduing the Tamil king, Elara, ruler of the sacred city of Anuradhapura. "Not for the joy of sovereignty is this toil of mine," Duttagamani declares. Rather, it is "ever to establish the doctrine of the Sambuddha."[48]

Notably, the *Mahavamsa* disregards the classical Buddhist emphasis on nonviolence and on the requirement that monks forswear war and politics. Duttagamani is described as carrying a relic of the Buddha into battle, and he enlists hundreds of monks to fight in his ranks. Most remarkably, when Duttagamani suffers remorse over his responsibility for slaying "millions of beings," he is reassured by a group of monks that his offense was trivial. To be precise, he had in fact killed only one-and-a-half human beings. One was a fairly advanced Buddhist, and the other—the "half human"—but a novice. All the others were non-Buddhists and of no account.

They were "unbelievers and men of evil life," "not more to be esteemed than beasts."[49] Besides, all that really mattered was that Duttagamani glorified the doctrine of the Buddha by restoring it to political dominance. He did that both by reasserting Sinhala Buddhist political control, and by vigorously undertaking to promote the cause of the Theravada sangha.

There was, in short, much in the Duttagamani epic, and in the warrior king and hero cult tradition celebrated by the *Mahavamsa*, that fit in with Dharmapala's version of Buddhist revivalism. Duttagamani stands in the grand tradition of defending the faith, by violence if necessary, that was supposedly initiated by Buddha himself.[50] There is, in particular, a close parallel between Buddha's expelling the alien Yakkhas and the Nagas by terror and Duttagamani's brutal victory over the Tamils. Dharmapala's basic vision of all this is captured in a passage from a thirteenth-century Sinhala work he loved to quote:

> This island belongs to the Buddha himself. . . . Therefore, the residence of wrong-believers in this Island will never be permanent, just as the residence of the Yakkhas of old was not permanent. Even if a non-Buddhist ruled Ceylon by force for a while, it is a particular power of the Buddha that his line will not be established. *Therefore, as Lanka is suitable only for Buddhist kings, it is certain that their lines, too, will be established.*[51]

On the other hand, however much these themes of heroes and warrior kings may have resonated in Dharmapala's time, and however much they may have been conveniently reappropriated in the struggle against western religion and western domination, they were nevertheless revised and reconstructed in certain ways to make them fit the imperatives of modern nationalism.

When, for instance, Dharmapala spoke of Vijaya, the founding father of Sri Lanka, as the progenitor of the "Aryan" Sinhala people,[52] he drew in the element of race in a novel way. This emphasis on the Sinhala as "a unique race," one "in whose veins no savage blood is found," has no anticipation or support in the *Mahavamsa*. Dharmapala clearly read

his late-nineteenth-century and early-twentieth-century views
back into the chronicles. His images were of course not
complete fabrications. The heroic tradition of the *Mahavamsa*
did lay great emphasis on Buddhist unity and dominance,
and that emphasis could be of use to an ultra-nationalist
such as Dharmapala. But the epics of Vijaya and Duttagamani
had to be recast in new dress before they could fully serve
the cause of modern nationalism. Dharmapala's inventive
role is unmistakable.[53]

Nor was race the only point of innovation. Dharmapala
and his fellow revivalists had little sensitivity to the important differences between modern forms of political culture
and organization and those characteristic of the *Mahavamsa*.
They thus inferred a degree of political and ethnic continuity
between past and present that did not exist.

Political unity and religious dominance looked one way
in ancient and medieval times and quite another in Dharmapala's world of burgeoning nation-states. Under premodern conditions, political arrangements, including those in Sri
Lanka, were generally "segmentary." Whatever political and
religious center might exist, as in the city kingdoms of
Anuradhapura and Kandy, was more symbolic than real.
The outlying units of political and cultural life enjoyed considerable autonomy so long as the center received its due
share of ritual homage. Accordingly, there was substantial
latitude for minority life and self-direction throughout the
kingdom, whether with respect to language, religion, "race,"
or the administration of affairs.[54]

In fact, ethnic boundaries were typically "porous and in-
distinct."[55] Tamil-speakers served as soldiers and guards to
the Sinhala kings, and South Indian and Tamil civilization
exerted important architectural and artistic influence on the
buildings and statuary of sacred Sinhala cities. Moreover,
archaeological evidence reveals the ancient intermixture of
culture, religion, and language in those very areas that are
today considered the strongholds of unadulterated Sinhala
or Tamil life.[56] Perhaps most remarkable of all, the kingdom
of Kandy, usually thought to be the last bastion of pure

Sinhala Buddhist culture before it yielded to the British in 1815, "was ruled in its last years by a dynasty of Tamil-speaking kings . . . from . . . South India." These kings are said to have converted to Buddhism, and one of them even revived a Buddhist monastic order.[57]

Also, it must not be forgotten that premodern Sri Lanka, because of caste, was segmented in an hierarchical sense. However opposed to caste classical Buddhism may have been, the Buddhism of the chronicles does not disparage caste.[58] The whole idea of the warrior king, central to the *Mahavamsa*, is that only members of the warrior, or Kshatriya, caste "can be legitimate kings."[59] Indeed, in the *Mahavamsa*, Buddha himself becomes the prototypical warrior king.[60] His bellicose behavior in banishing the faithless and disreputable Yakkhas and Nagas from the face of Sri Lanka is consistent with his own Kshatriya origins. This reiteration of the importance of caste divisions reduced the impulse to unify all Sinhala into one inclusive whole. The stories of heroes such as Vijaya and Duttagamani could rally a degree of common political loyalty, but that common focus in no way threatened "the hierarchical morality of caste" or the "distinction between the polity and a variety of other groups—indigenous people, nonbelievers, low-castes, and South Indians."[61]

It is of course exactly this pattern of segmentation, of a disjointed arrangement of autonomous units and castes loosely attached to a symbolic center, that stands in such stark contrast to the modern political system emerging during Dharmapala's time. The nineteenth-century innovation associated with the rise of nationalism was, above all, "to rally the generality of the people—male and female, high and low—to a common cause."[62]

Nationalism radically transformed communities traditionally diffused and dispersed into consolidated, inclusive, standardized "mass societies" bound together by a shared sense of being a people, of having a distinctive national identity. How that process of consolidation took place is a familiar story: modern means of communication and transportation, emergence of mass politics and mass markets with elaborate bureaucratic and administrative structures, development of centrally controlled public education, and so forth.[63]

Dharmapala was a part of that transformation in Sri Lanka. It was he who skillfully gathered up the disparate expressions of anticolonialism "into a powerful and effective oppositional platform, *which was open to all Sinhala Buddhists, irrespective of their primary caste, class and regional affiliations.*"[64] In Dharmapala's hands and those of his fellow revivalists, the ancient theme of unity among ruler, sangha, and Sinhala people—a theme only partially and selectively implemented in premodern times—was transmuted into a program capable of generating a new all-embracing ethnic consciousness and mobilizing support for a political system dominated by that ethnic consciousness. In short, Dharmapala and his associates very much encouraged and contributed to something aptly called the "ethnocratic state."[65]

### Sinhala Buddhism Reconstituted

More precisely, Dharmapala "gave contemporary meaning to two fundamental concerns which are evident in the history of the Sinhala": first, the anxiety, classically expressed by Duttagamani's contorted position on his bed, that the Sinhala are a beleaguered people, a people hemmed in and threatened by menacing hordes of South Indians just off their shores as well as by British intruders and other "barbaric vandals"; second, the imperative to withstand—*"be it by the use of force"*—the dire threat posed by these sworn enemies to the historic mission of the Sinhala, the protection of Buddhism.[66]

In mobilizing the Sinhala, Dharmapala undertook to reform both the monks and the laity.[67] The monks, he felt, had in general lost their vision and sense of mission. They either had yielded to a life of ease or, in their preoccupation with meditation and striving for salvation, were overly isolated from their urgent social responsibilities. The Christian missionaries may have been misguided in many ways, but they knew what self-sacrifice and dedication meant in the cause of rebuilding society. The monks could learn from the missionaries.

Above all, it was time for the monks to forsake their passive lives and rural hideaways. They should become missionaries to foreign lands, like India and Burma, as Dharmapala himself had done. Or they should live in the cities of Sri Lanka actively propagating their message in lively encounter with the people. In either case, they must recommit themselves to the ascetic life, the life of renunciation, characteristic of authentic Buddhism. But they must channel the energy that flows from such commitment into social encounter and reform, even "at the expense of salvation-striving."[68] Thus, was the "political bhikkhu" born, a religious militant who would come to play an important role in the twentieth-century revival of Sinhala Buddhism.[69]

Dharmapala refashioned the image of the Buddhist layperson in a similar way. Disregarding the traditional conception of the laity as peripheral to achieving salvation, he sought "to build a tightly knit, well-disciplined Buddhist congregation with a common corpus of belief and awareness of its strength as a politico-religious group."[70] Like the monk, the layperson must recover Buddhist doctrine and practice and must submit to the laws of discipline. Toward that end, Dharmapala worked out a "Daily Code for the Laity," consisting of 200 rules that covered eating, dress, hygiene, domestic duties, social conduct, the naming and rearing of children, religious practices, and so on.[71] Not only does this code symbolize Dharmapala's concern to inspire this-worldly asceticism among laypeople, it also represents his effort to consolidate an inclusive Sinhala society with a new ethnic consciousness. The code constituted "a common platform cutting across caste and kin lines and eliminating village cultural practices which had a specific regional or caste focus."[72]

## The New Intolerance

The upshot of Buddhist revivalism, represented by Anagarika Dharmapala, was to provide a warrant for intolerance, for viewing as inferiors and discriminating against peoples "perceived as obstacles to what rightfully belongs to the Sinhala."[73]

There are precedents for such intolerance within the chronicle tradition. But the particular character and intensity of Dharmapala's intolerance depended on special religious, cultural, and political conditions and influences in the nineteenth and early twentieth centuries. To that extent, Dharmapala's intolerance was "invented" or "new."

One of the earlier and more virulent manifestations of this new intolerance occurred in 1915 against some Sri Lankan Muslims. They were active and successful retail traders and became the target of their frustrated Sinhala competitors. Dharmapala, whose father was one of those frustrated competitors, took up the cause of the Sinhala merchants. In 1906, he joined a number of writers, dramatists, journalists, and monks in celebrating the victories of Duttagamani and other heroic rulers over foreign invaders and traders:

> Aliens are taking away the wealth of the country; and the sons of the soil, where are they to go? The immigrants who came here have other places to go, the Sinhala has no place to go. Is it just that the sons of the soil should suffer while the alien enjoy? . . . The ignorant helpless Sinhala villager is made a victim by the alien sharper who robs his ancestral land.[74]

Dharmapala's antipathy deepened after he spent some time in India, especially in Bengal, where a new militancy among Indian nationalists fired his imagination. Upon his return to Sri Lanka in 1912, he "started [the] National revival and toured all over Ceylon,"[75] applying some of the lessons he had learned in Bengal, particularly the use of the boycott against foreign products. By this time, he had begun to single out the Muslim traders:

> The Muhammedans, an alien people, . . . by shylockian methods became prosperous like the Jews. The Sinhala sons of the soil, whose ancestors for 2358 years had shed rivers of blood to keep the country free of alien invaders . . . are in the eyes of the British only vagabonds. . . . The alien South Indian Muhammedan comes to Ceylon, sees the neglected villager, without any experience in trade . . . and the result is that the Muhammedan thrives and the sons of the soil go to the wall.[76]

Religious and ethnic antagonism of this sort "gave a sharp ideological focus and a cloak of respectability to sordid commercial rivalry" between the groups.[77] In the riots that occurred, hundreds were killed or injured, and there was considerable property damage. In fact, so destructive was the outcome that the British grew anxious. They suspected the violence was more than intercommunal strife. To them, it bore the marks of Sinhala anticolonial nationalism reminiscent of what was occurring in India, and they imposed martial law promptly and severely. They imprisoned suspected nationalist leaders, condemning several of them to death. Two of Dharmapala's brothers were detained, and one died in jail after his death sentence had been commuted. Some editors whose newspapers had published anti-Muslim diatribes were prosecuted, and Dharmapala's *Sinhala Bauddhaya* was banned.

Though anticolonialism in Sri Lanka never became as militant or resolute as it did in India, 1915 was a turning point for the Sinhala. They lost confidence in the probity and impartiality of the British, who refused to investigate charges that their response to the riots had been excessive and abusive.[78] A month after the riots, Dharmapala expressed the rage of the Sinhala in telling words:

> What the German is to the Britisher . . . the Muhammedan is to the Sinhala. He is alien to the Sinhala by religion, race and language. . . . To the Sinhala without Buddhism death is preferable. The British officials may shoot, hang, quarter, imprison or do anything to the Sinhala but there will always be bad blood between the Moors and the Sinhala. The peaceful Sinhala have at last shown that they can no longer bear the insults of the alien. The whole nation in one day has risen against the Moor people. The causes are economic and spiritual.[79]

Training the full force of such rhetoric against the Tamils was the next step. That was achieved not so much by Dharmapala, who died in 1933, as by other Buddhist revivalists who followed him and whom he influenced. To be sure, Dharmapala himself was hardly above including references to "filthy Tamils" among his continuing diatribes against the "exploiting" Muslims as well as against the "meat-eating, low caste" Christians.[80] But although he was not responsible for perfecting the crusade against the Tamils that came to its climax in the 1950s, he clearly laid the groundwork for that crusade. Dharmapala provided all the essential premises: the racial and religious purity and superiority of the Sinhala; their incontestable sacred and historic right to rule; the need to contain and control the always menacing, barely tolerable non-Sinhala minorities on the island. It was just this mix of ancient myth and modern resentment that could give authority to the impulse to create a Sinhala ethnocracy in Sri Lanka.

In the last analysis, the revivalists had no room in their thinking for a multiethnic society in which all groups were regarded as equal. Dharmapala and his associates capitalized, in effect, on one fundamental point: "In the Sinhala language, the words for nation, race and people are practically synonymous, and a multiethnic or multicommunal nation or state is incomprehensible to the popular mind. *The emphasis on Sri Lanka as the land of the Sinhala Buddhists carried an emotional popular appeal, compared with which the concept of a multiethnic polity was a meaningless abstraction.*"[81]

*four*

# The Tamil Response

## South Indian Nationalism and Sri Lankan Separatism

The case is made that, for their part, the Tamils became gripped by the same kind of "narrow and parochial chauvinism" as the Sinhala and that these convictions influenced the spirit of Tamil separatism.[1] The case is less complete and more controversial than for the Sinhala, and it calls for further exploration.[2] The argument is that Tamil revivalism was in many ways the mirror image of Sinhala revivalism. "The two [movements] are broadly alike in their character, fervor and their Christian roots," and they play a similar role in fostering "ethnic antagonism" and mutual intolerance.[3] The movements are alike because to a certain degree the Tamils imitated the Sinhala revivalists and because both movements responded to the same historical conditions and influences. In addition, Tamil grievances over perceived mistreatment by the majority intensified their ethnocentrism.[4]

### The "Christian Roots" of South Indian Nationalism

If both movements have Christian roots, there is nevertheless a certain difference. The "missionary factor" had a generally negative effect on the development of Sinhala identity. Missionary aggressiveness and condescension eventually incited a Buddhist counteroffensive. But the effects of the missionaries on the Tamils were more complex. The claim is that missionaries were not just an irritant, not just an object of hostility, as in the Sinhala case, but that they encouraged and made constructive contributions to Tamil revivalism.[5] By stimulating the rise of South Indian nationalism in the nineteenth and early twentieth centuries, Christian missionaries gave indirect impetus to Sri Lankan Tamil nationalism, which was an offshoot of the Indian movement.[6]

Through his pioneering philological work, the Reverend Robert Caldwell (1819–91), a Protestant missionary, became no less than "the founder of . . . South Indian . . . nationalism."[7] Caldwell contended that there was a fundamental difference between North and South Indians, between "Aryan" or "Brahman" and "Dravidian" or Tamil language and culture. What is more, the latter are easily equal, if not superior, to the former.

Other missionaries and British colonial officials joined Caldwell in defending the "elegance and sophistication" of Dravidian language and literature against the assumption that the Sanskrit tradition, the pride of the north, alone constituted the standard of excellence for all of India. The same was true, they believed, of the idea that the Brahman caste is the pinnacle of society. They regarded Dravidian religion—a branch of Hinduism called Saiva Siddhanta—as a distinct and profound spiritual expression,[8] and they disparaged the inclination of the northerners to look down on the mostly non-Brahman southerners as "low caste." One official, J. H. Nelson, wrote a book in 1868 supporting Caldwell's ideas and arguing that non-Brahmans were actually superior to Brahmans.[9]

All this led to an indigenous literary and cultural movement among the Tamils dedicated to the antiquity, originality, and preeminence of Dravidian culture. "Most of what is ignorantly called Aryan philosophy, Aryan civilization, is literally Dravidian or Tamilian at bottom," as one revivalist put it in the early twentieth century.[10] Any abiding tokens of Sanskrit culture and Brahman religion evident in the south existed not because of intrinsic appeal, but because of a long and mournful record of northern intrusion and repression.

In the early twentieth century, new groups—such as the Justice Party, the Madras Presidency Association, and the Self-respect Movement—gave social and political expression to resentment by the South Indians toward what they felt were policies of domination by the north that relegated them to an inferior status. These groups celebrated Tamil history and culture and rebelled against the lowly status ascribed to them by Brahmanism. They assigned themselves a more elevated position in the caste structure and set about reclaiming their tradition. Among other things, they demanded that more attention be given in schools to indigenous classics, to consideration of Saiva Siddhanta, and to Dravidian languages.

A specific aim of the Self-respect Movement was "to remove 'Aryan' elements from the culture and day to day behavior of the Dravidians, which amounted, all over again, to a denial of Brahman superiority."[11] Wedding ceremonies dispensed with the services of Brahman priests, and there were public burnings of "Aryan" religious texts. The movement gave rise to a popular newspaper, *People's Government*, which represented Brahmans as "usurper lords." In addition, the Self-respect Movement, like other groups, gave expression to strong resentment among South Indians toward perceived social, economic, and educational discrimination at the hands of the Brahmans.[12]

These groups resisted the idea of Indian home rule, advocated by Gandhi and others, seeing it as a scheme to perpetuate Brahman dominance. Increasingly "radical and intolerant" in the 1930s, they adopted the slogan "Tamil Nadu for the Tamilians," demanding that India be divided into three separate states—Aryan, Muslim, and Dravidian— and by 1949, the Justice Party was devoting itself entirely to the creation of a separate Tamil state. "This constitutes the logical conclusion of the notions of territorial, racial, religious and cultural purity and exclusivity imagined in the scholarly treatises dealing with the Tamil past."[13]

## The Sri Lankan Tamil Connection

"Tamil nationalism in Jaffna cannot be seen as separate from Tamil nationalism in south India by which it has been influenced and on which it has, to some extent, fed."[14] Two reasons are suggested why Sri Lankan Tamils came to identify with South Indian revivalism.[15] There were, of course, the close linguistic, social, and cultural links to South India. For example, since nearly all Hindus in Sri Lanka are adherents of Saiva Siddhanta, they naturally "have looked to South India for religious and cultural inspiration."[16] Sri Lankan Tamils have frequently made pilgrimages to South India, and religious dignitaries from the south have regularly visited the Jaffna area. South Indian revivalism, with its intense religious concerns, could be expected to have repercussions in Sri Lanka.

Moreover, the way the Sinhala revivalists pictured and projected themselves tended to remind their Tamil compatriots of the conflict between North and South India. Except that their religion was Buddhist and not Brahman, the Sinhala fashioned themselves in a North Indian likeness. They were supposed to be Aryans; their language was derived from Sanskrit; they were allegedly born to rule.[17] Not surprisingly, Sri Lankan Tamils responded by comparing themselves to their South Indian counterparts and by using against the Sinhala methods of retaliation refined by the South Indians.[18]

The life and work of the influential Hindu revivalist Arumuga Navalar (1822–78) illustrate the natural ties between Tamil nationalists in South India and those in Sri Lanka. A distinguished literary scholar and educator from Jaffna, Navalar spent thirty years attempting to recover and disseminate the teachings of Saiva Siddhanta, and other Tamil literature, in Sri Lanka as well as in South India.[19] His appeal as "the champion reformer of the Hindus" and "the father of modern Tamil prose" was readily transferable from one place to the other,[20] as were the effects of his work in renovating and restoring Hindu temples.

All of Navalar's work bears a polemical edge, pertinent to both India and Sri Lanka. In a typical presentation, he would explain to his audience that those who follow the Vedas, or sacred texts of Brahmanism, "will attain merit, but those who follow the Saiva Path will attain salvation."[21] On other occasions, he would inveigh against Brahman rituals and urge the people not to allow Brahmans to perform ceremonies unless the Brahmans brought their practices more into line with Saiva teaching.[22] Predictably, Brahmans were offended by Navalar's relentless animadversions.

Navalar's educational work in Sri Lanka provides another example of his assertiveness. His remarkable achievements were all motivated by a passion to break the missionary monopoly over the schools in the Tamil area. He wanted to reduce what he took to be alien cultural and religious domination by Christians, no doubt reminiscent, in his mind, of the domineering style of Brahman culture in India. He went some distance toward his goal of establishing "Saivite schools in every [Tamil] village," and he succeeded in founding the Jaffna Hindu College. The Society for the Propagation of Saivism, better known as the Hindu Board of Education, was a result of Navalar's efforts, and it eventually brought about a substantial increase in the number of Hindu schools in northern Sri Lanka. But all this was accomplished against bitter opposition from the missionaries, opposition even more ferocious than was visited on the Buddhists in the south.[23]

As for the basis of Tamil claims for an autonomous homeland in Sri Lanka, it is suggested that "the answer lies in the Dravidian movement in South India, the loftiest goal of which was the establishment of the promised land of Dravidastan or Dravidanad."[24] Just as South Indian nationalists believed themselves entitled to reestablish the ancient Dravidian kingdom, so Sri Lankan Tamils claimed such a right on the strength of their conviction that "a sovereign Tamil state was in existence in Sri Lanka from prehistoric times."[25]

According to the Sri Lankan Tamils, Tamil rule in Sri Lanka was very ancient, though the extent of Tamil control in the struggle against the Sinhala fluctuated constantly for more than a thousand years, depending on the fortunes of war. Then, during the thirteenth century, a separate, sovereign

Tamil kingdom was consolidated, covering about half the island and including the northern, northwestern, and eastern sections. The Portuguese conquered that kingdom in the sixteenth century and were followed eventually by the British, who subsumed it in the larger colony of Ceylon.[26] It seemed self-evident to the Sri Lankan Tamils, as it had to the South Indians, that with the termination of British rule and the end of colonialism the country ought to revert to its time-honored patterns of ethnically divided governance.

The Sri Lankan Tamils attempted to shore up their historical claims to a homeland with supplementary appeals similar to those employed by the South Indian nationalists.[27] Until about the 1930s, they "tried to prove that the Sinhala were in reality not Aryans, but Dravidians in disguise, and thus had nothing to be snooty about."[28] But after 1930, the mood changed. Sri Lankan Tamils began to sound a more ethnocentric note: "The Ceylon Tamils were the original inhabitants of this island and the Sinhalese people of old had regarded themselves as an off-shoot of the Tamil nation."[29] Support for that conviction was along the following lines:

> According to tradition, the Tamils of India and Sri Lanka are the lineal descendants of the Naga and [Yakkha] people. . . . Nagadipa in the north of Sri Lanka was an actual kingdom . . . and the people who occupied it were all part of an immigrant tribe from South India, Tamil people called Nagas. . . . [T]he ancestors of the present day Tamils were the original occupiers of the island long before 543 BC which the Pali chronicles date as the earliest human habitation in Sri Lanka.[30]

This interpretation is remarkably at odds with the use made of "the Pali chronicles" by the Sinhala revivalists. For Dharmapala, the Nagas and Yakkhas were subhuman and malevolent, an abiding threat to the virtue and stability represented by Vijaya and the Sinhala. Their expulsion from Sri Lanka by the Buddha was fully justified. For Tamil revivalists, the argument is just the opposite: If the Nagas and the Yakkhas were not after all subhuman, but ordinary South Indians, as they believed, then the real founders of Sri Lankan civilization were the Tamils, and "theirs was the highest culture . . . from which others only copied, and everything great and good in both Sri Lanka and Sinhala culture was by definition originally Tamil."[31]

Nor did this viewpoint apply only to language, literature, and architecture. It also applied to religion: "Attempts were made to prove that the Sinhala, far from being Buddhists, were in reality Hindus, or that Buddhism was just an inferior kind of Hinduism." If Tamils were not to be given the dominant place in Sri Lanka (which this kind of thinking implied they deserved), they ought at least to be considered on an equal footing with the Sinhala.[32]

The South Indian–Sri Lankan Tamil connection would also explain why many South Indian Tamils continue to support the establishment of a separate state in Sri Lanka.[33] "Although separatist sentiment still lives in South India, it is at present unlikely to yield a separate state. On the other hand, Sri Lanka, with its geographical and cultural proximity to South India and its Tamil minority more numerically strong than anywhere else, is the most likely location for the realization of Eelam."[34]

### The Impact of Modern Nationalism

The impulses of modern nationalism had much the same effect on Tamil revivalism that they had on Sinhala revivalism. Tamil nationalists of the nineteenth and twentieth centuries were just as liable as their Sinhala counterparts to distort the crucial difference between the modern and the premodern world.

Like Dharmapala and his associates, Tamil nationalists viewed ancient and medieval society in India and Sri Lanka through the lens of the nation-state. In their ardor to base the policies of the present on the precedents of the past, they mistook the segmentary political arrangements that actually existed, arrangements with "floating rather than fixed" boundaries, with relatively amorphous and variable lines of authority, and with considerable local autonomy and ethnic heterogeneity. Instead they saw modern-looking states where sovereignty was "absolute, indivisible and inalienable, and ... territorial integrity ... inviolable."[35] For the Tamils, like the Sinhala, these mythical projections became the warrant for modern nationalism.

### Special Circumstances

But with all the similarities, Sri Lankan Tamils are still distinguishable from South Indians in some respects.[36] They may be Tamils, but they are also Sri Lankans. Ironically, it is the special connection, the shared history, with the Sinhala, however estranged the two groups might be, that in the end differentiates the Tamil community in Sri Lanka from that in South India and gives it a residual "identity of its own."[37] Unlike the South Indians, Sri Lankan Tamils are distinctive for being "prey to ... double alienation."[38] They feel peripheral or marginal in relation both to the Sinhala and to the South Indians, a condition that compounds their sense of frustration and distress and intensifies their longing for a homeland.[39]

This condition is particularly acute, it is suggested, for Sri Lankan Tamil expatriates. They have an especially strong ideological attachment to the idea of a Holy Land, and they see themselves as living for the time being in diaspora. "This is quite understandable when we consider the fact that [Sri Lankan] Tamil communities exist in South India, Malaysia, and more recently in other parts of the world, but nowhere are they in a majority.... [T]hey perceive themselves as an oppressed group."[40] Consequently, the expatriates are disposed to contribute financial support to militant Sri Lankan Tamil separatists in what are widely considered to be "staggering amounts."[41]

## How Deep Is the South Indian–Sri Lankan Connection?

Viewed from another perspective, the link between South Indian revivalism and Sri Lankan separatism appears somewhat far-fetched. It is not denied that the Dravidian movement stood in the background of Tamil nationalism, and it may even have had some special impact on the Sri Lankan Tamil community after 1956.[42] But there is reason to doubt whether it played "in any way a dominant role."[43]

There are several objections. First, Jaffna Tamil leaders of the early twentieth century did not typically dwell on their Dravidian roots. Many of them may have gone back and forth between Jaffna and South India, participating in political life in both places, but their two-way access was a result more of colonial ties between South India and Sri Lanka than of a common culture. Moreover, the early founders of separatist ideology were not Hindus at all, but "good Jaffna Christians."[44]

Second, the anti-Brahman aspect of the Dravidian movement in South India had only "the faintest resonance" in Jaffna, since there were so few Brahmans there.[45] The same is true of the "purist" impulse to purge Sanskrit and Aryan elements from Tamil language and culture. Jaffna writers and poets cared little about that.

Third, Dravidian revivalism in South India was actually more concerned with political and economic redress against the Brahmans than with cultural purity. No sooner had Brahman domination in South India been undermined in the 1960s than Dravidian revivalists "abandoned all the anti-Brahman, anti-Aryan, anti–North Indian" elements, particularly the earlier attack on religion and ritual.[46]

Fourth, whatever the degree of cultural reform achieved by Tamils in South India and Sri Lanka, it had very little impact on politics. The continuity that does exist between state and religion in Buddhism does not apply in the same way in Tamil society and culture.[47] Dravidian revivalism did not readily translate into reformist political schemes.

A more likely source of Sri Lankan separatism, it is suggested, is the special set of circumstances in Sri Lanka in which the Tamil community found itself. Tamil separatism is "mainly a reactive movement," something fashioned in response to local events and local traditions rather than primarily a result of external cultural influences.[48]

According to this argument, Sri Lankan Tamils believe they possess a firm historical title to a certain share of the island. "Tamils have been [here] from time immemorial," controlling and administering territories that were expropriated under colonialism. With the departure of the British, it is only "proper that the status quo ante be reestablished."[49] Despite appearances, this is not a revivalist argument. It does not legitimate itself in a pan-Tamil spirit but rests its case on legalistic appeals entirely specific to Sri Lanka.

Historical justifications for a separate homeland have been supplemented by two other considerations. One is the perception of "systematic discrimination against Tamils" by the Sinhala majority, particularly after the 1950s.[50] The second is a claim to the right of conquest. "Tamil militants claimed they fought for this land and won it and according to the rights of victors they are entitled to rule it." The land "has now been rendered sacred by the amount of Tamil blood spilled to secure it." As one Tamil patriot has said, "It is too late to settle for a unitary state with Tamil rights guaranteed. Even if the Sinhala grant all the demands we made earlier, too much blood has been spilled. We cannot settle for anything less than a separate state."[51]

## A Variety of Responses?

It seems reasonable that the arguments of the Sri Lankan Tamils for separating themselves from the Sinhala majority are not all of a piece. Different arguments might be deployed at different times and under different circumstances. Perhaps *both* the South Indian context *and* local Sri Lankan conditions are important, depending on time and place.[52]

> Tamil historical consciousness, and the resulting Tamil nationalism, is not simply "reactive," a product of Tamil responses to Sinhala chauvinism and the Sinhala emphasis on their own history. Tamil nationalism in Jaffna cannot be seen as separate from Tamil nationalism in south India by which it has been influenced and on which it has, to some extent, fed. But what Sinhala nationalism and historical awareness brought about

was *a heightened sense of being Jaffna Tamil instead of just Tamil, thus leading to a withdrawal from the wider context of subcontinental Tamil culture and history.*[53]

Another account makes similar room for different responses at different times.[54] It is suggested that recently, "the discourse of a chosen people, which is a familiar and important part of Sinhalese nationalism, has become a new and disturbing phenomenon in Tamil political writing." Some of that Sinhala nationalism can be traced to South Indian "anti-Brahman, populist nationalism," which "had an important effect on Sri Lankan Tamil consciousness in the 50s and 60s." At the same time, there was no automatic influence. Some Sri Lankan Tamils, who were drawn to the Dravidian movement and to Saiva Siddhanta consciousness, were actually on the fringes. The main Tamil political leaders of the period were Christians and therefore were not touched by South Indian nationalism. Nor were Tamil demands for a separate state in the 1970s oriented toward Dravidian nationalism. They were "centered around Tamil grievances based on linguistic and territorial rights and their sense of oppression."

However, 1983 marked a radical change. "Certain Tamil nationalist myths which had been politically latent began to be openly expressed; there was a deliberate and conscious attempt to create a Dravida, Saiva Siddhanta political identity." Interestingly, the impulse for this came not so much from Madras or Jaffna, "but from the expatriate community, who have begun to write extensively on Tamil history and ideology. Their writings are circulated widely and have an important effect on Tamil consciousness."[55]

# PART II:

# PATTERNS OF CONFLICT

*five*

# The Failure of "Premature and Artificial Cosmopolitanism"[1]

## Pluralism on Trial

In 1956, eight years after independence, Solomon West Ridgeway Dias Bandaranaike and his newly formed Sri Lanka Freedom Party swept into power, overturning the United National Party and many of the ideals that had been laid down by the country's first prime minister, Don Stephen Senanayake, before his death in 1952. In a profound sense Bandaranaike's victory "was a significant turning point in Sri Lanka's history."[2] It retarded severely the attempt to fashion an integrated, multiethnic Sri Lanka based on equal freedom and tolerance for all and substituted a divisive form of "populist nationalism" redolent of the spirit of revivalism. Thereafter, civil peace and harmony in Sri Lanka would be difficult to come by.

### A Model Postcolonial Leader

Senanayake appeared to fit perfectly the needs of latter-day colonialism. As the British began to think the unthinkable in the first quarter or so of the twentieth century—that independence and self-government for the colonies was the wave of the future—they set about nurturing an indigenous political system and governing class that could at the appropriate time be trusted to carry on in the best British tradition. Indeed, what was tried in Sri Lanka set the standard for the independence process in many other colonies.[3]

Up to a point, Senanayake allied himself closely with British objectives.[4] Born of an upper class family who made considerable wealth in coconuts and graphite, he was educated in the liberal, multiethnic atmosphere typical, in the early twentieth century, of the prestigious schools modeled on the British public school. More at home in English than in their indigenous languages and identified more by school ties than by ethnic consciousness, he and his classmates— Sinhala and Tamil alike—inclined to disdain as bad form all indications of communalism. This elite group, never more than 4 percent of the population,[5] were being groomed as leaders with a pragmatic and secular disposition, suspicious of primordial attachments of any kind, and sufficiently flexible and worldly-wise to cope with the complicated demands of modern democracy.

Aside from an early brush or two with the colonial authorities—once as the leader of a Buddhist-inspired temperance movement against the liquor trade—Senanayake cooperated with the British throughout his years in politics and public service, beginning in the 1920s. Overall, he was

> much more sensitive than the majority of his colleagues and associates in the national leadership to the political implications that flowed from the plural nature of Sri Lankan society, and showed greater concern for political and constitutional concessions to the minorities to win their support for a joint program of action on the transfer of power. Thus he readily accepted the proposition that the Sri Lankan polity would hold no special privileges for any single ethnic group.[6]

### Liabilities

Senanayake believed with the British that the Donoughmore Constitution, recommended by a commission of distinguished Britons and adopted in 1931, offered an opportunity to minimize ethnic tension in the process of advancing democracy and moving toward self-determination. The constitution introduced several radical electoral and parliamentary reforms, the most important of which was universal suffrage.[7] The idea was to eliminate the established system of communal representation, which in the minds of the commission simply intensified ethnic division.

In promoting the reforms, Senanayake and his fellow adherents had to withstand substantial opposition. Some Sinhala rejected it, presumably for fear that the new system would disrupt favorable voting patterns. For their part, the minorities, especially the Tamils, were horrified. Majority rule spelled Sinhala rule so far as they were concerned. The Donoughmore Constitution threatened the delicate communal political balance worked out under colonial authority. That arrangement had yielded disproportionately generous opportunities for the Tamil elite and, in a general way, had appeared to the Tamils and other minorities to modify invidious distinctions between majority and minority.[8]

Throughout the 1930s and 1940s, Tamil leaders, in occasional league with the Muslims, offered several counterproposals, seeking in various ways to provide guarantees and safeguards against what they perceived as the danger of majority dictatorship. One such proposal—the so-called fifty-fifty campaign—involved a complicated system of special electoral adjustments that would prevent any one ethnic group from outvoting a combination of the others. This arrangement, along with certain modifications, was debated throughout the 1930s, but was not in the end acceptable to the Sinhala, to the colonial authorities, or even to all members of the minority communities.

The great fear of the colonial authorites, a fear shared by Senanayake, was that any form of "fractional representation on a race basis," "any concession to the principle of communal representation," "would perpetuate sectionalism" and retard the development of a modern multiethnic society in Sri Lanka.[9] Sinhala politicians, along with the members of the Donoughmore Commission, believed "special pleading for minority 'communal' privileges was a case of self-interested obstruction of progress and of [the] march toward self-government."[10] The fact that the Tamils boycotted the elections in 1931 that were authorized by the new consititution "confirmed in Sinhalese eyes [Tamil] willingness to impede the political advance of Ceylon by placing their minority privileges before the national interest."[11]

Certain minor electoral adjustments were eventually admitted in an attempt to reduce minority apprehension. Furthermore, the procedures of appointment and decision making that constituted the principal executive committee under Donoughmore were believed, with some justification, "to encourage a spirit of compromise" that might reduce antagonism among the representatives of the various communities.[12]

However, notwithstanding the optimism of Senanayake and the colonial authorities, minority worries were, after all, well founded. None of this procedural tinkering could overcome the powerful combination of "arithmetical politics" and the "communalist virus" that had already worked its way deep into the Sri Lankan body politic. So long as the British managed the island, Donoughmore gave the appearance of providing a relatively balanced and impartial system under the terms of universal suffrage. But once the British left, there was little to prevent the dominant Sinhala community, driven as it was by growing ethnocentrism, from taking advantage of its sizable electoral strength, just as the minorities had predicted.[13]

Nor did the subsequent legal and political charter—the Soulbury Constitution of 1947, which laid down the terms of decolonization and self-government and which bore Senanayake's unmistakable imprint—achieve much better results in inoculating Sri Lanka against the communalist virus.

To be sure, with Senanayake's encouragement, the Soulbury Constitution extended concessions begun under Donoughmore, such as special electoral weighting on behalf of the minorities.[14] Nevertheless, taken as a whole, Soulbury had the effect of evading the ethnic realities of Sri Lanka. It assumed "the possibility of communal harmony without supportive institutional procedures."[15] The commission that drafted it "never urged [an out-and-out] negotiated settlement between the Sinhalese and Tamil communities" to create "a framework for a national accord," nor "did they set in motion a tradition of accommodation and negotiation between the two major ethnic groups." If anything, the end result of their efforts was to "set one group against the other in competition for favours."[16]

Specifically, the Soulbury Constitution enshrined without much qualification the principles of unitary government and majoritarian rule. The consequence was a highly centralized bureaucratic and political system with inadequate protection for basic rights,[17] particularly minority rights.[18] The drafting commission staunchly resisted the idea of a bill of rights. The British did not need one; why should the Sri Lankans?[19] Even Senanayake, who started out opposing that view in the interest of further reassuring the Tamils, "was dissuaded from supporting [a bill of rights] by the arguments of his principal advisor on constitutional affairs, Sir Ivor Jennings, for whom the applicability of the Westminster constitutional model to the Sri Lankan situation was an article of faith."[20]

Section 29(2) of the Soulbury Constitution prohibited legislation that infringed on the religious freedom of any citizen or discriminated against persons of any community or religion. But in the face of the vigorous resurgence of Sinhala nationalism that was about to appear, this section would prove a weak reed. Much more elaboration of basic protections was needed, including, most importantly, provisions for a robust and independent judiciary. "Without the anchor of a Bill of Rights, the possibility of an activist judiciary as a vehicle of social reform was rendered remote."[21]

### Senanayake's Other Side

Dramatic and surprising evidence that the British woefully underestimated the virulence of ethnic tension in Sri Lanka is manifest, as a matter of fact, in one of Senanayake's own early policies as prime minister, initiated just after independence. Through a series of legislative acts, the new Senanayake administration disenfranchised and denied citizenship to virtually all the nearly one million Indian resident laborers whom the British, beginning in the nineteenth century, had brought in from South India to work on the newly developed tea and coffee plantations in central Sri Lanka. These people are known as Indian or Estate Tamils as distinct from Ceylon or Sri Lankan Tamils. The two groups have never been close, and in fact some Sri Lankan Tamil politicians at the time revealed their own contempt toward the immigrant population by voting with Senanayake in favor of the legislation.[22]

Still, Senanayake's own motivation was not free of a residual Sinhala prejudice, even for one as liberated as he.[23] By disqualifying so large a portion of the non-Sinhala electorate, Senanayake had given a huge political advantage to the Sinhala community. It would now be much easier for the Sinhala to obtain two-thirds majorities in the parliament and thereby to gain effective dominance over the country.[24] The consequences for ethnic relations of Senanayake's legislation on the "Indian question" were not hard to foresee.[25]

Indeed, in providing a general assessment of Senanayake's role as one of the founders of modern Sri Lanka, his "western cosmopolitan" orientation should not perhaps be overemphasized. The influence of Sinhala Buddhism on his outlook appears to have been important. He was, for example, "the first modern Sri Lankan politician to identify himself with ancient kings and traditional practices."[26] In keeping with the inclinations of his family, he traced his descent to Parakramabahu I, a medieval warrior king, idolized in the chronicles. Parakramabahu, or "strong arm," unified Sri Lanka under Buddhism. He recovered the holy city of Anuradhapura as the center of the kingdom, reformed the monasteries, and built the Temple of the Tooth Relic, though he is particularly remembered for the elaborate irrigation works he constructed.[27]

Senanayake patterned himself after King Parakramabahu. He showed strong interest in monastic schools, and in 1947, attired in national dress and white shawl, he prostrated himself before a collection of Buddhist relics and then carried "the relic casket on his head on behalf of the Buddhist public."[28] By such acts, Senanayake "initiated the process that has culminated in the present-day practice by which elected leaders regularly show traditional forms of respect to Buddhism in public settings."[29]

In the late 1930s, under the Land Development Ordinance of 1935, Senanayake set about renovating the irrigation system in the northern and eastern provinces and opening up agricultural opportunities there, with the idea that "what our ancient kings had done the modern rulers could do equally well."[30] Developing land for cultivation in the so-called Dry Zone would enable landless Sinhala peasants to become independent property owners. Development would also relieve unemployment, increase food production, and establish new areas of prosperity.[31] The British had begun such policies, but Senanayake and his associates believed those initiatives worked against the special needs and interests of Sinhala peasants. Moreover, they recast the colonization program in accord with "millennial visions" that favored attempts to restore "the grandeur of what they conceived the island's past to be."[32] While minister of agriculture, Senanayake recalled in a speech that the Buddha himself had appointed the Sinhala to be custodians of the faith. As such, he said, "we are one blood and one nation. We are a chosen people."[33] Sentiments like these were "responsible for infusing Sinhalese nationalism" with new colonial aspirations.[34]

Senanayake's colonization program, possibly because it was couched so clearly in Sinhala nationalist terms, was a source of intense anxiety for the Tamils. Whether or not Tamil objections were justified,[35] the program was for that reason an important cause of deepening ethnic tension. Tamil leaders registered vigorous criticisms before the Soulbury Commission that the expansion of Sinhala settlements threatened the majority status of the Tamils in the northern and eastern sections of Sri Lanka.[36] After independence Tamil apprehension grew stronger, and that was one reason for the emergence of the Tamil Federal party

in 1949 and eventually for the movement in favor of a
separate state.[37]

### Fatal Flaw

No doubt the major reason Senanayake's brand of "secular
nationalism" failed in the end was its lack of widespread
popular support. It was "basically elitist in conception."[38]
Neither the British nor leaders such as Senanayake understood
the need to reach out beyond the upper stratum and begin
creating a new mass political culture that would acquaint
average citizens with the demands and responsibilities of
pluralist democracy.

Because of the elitism, Senanayake and his British sponsors
were out of touch; they did not appreciate what they were
up against. That explains their insensitivity to the burgeoning
power of ethnic nationalism in Sri Lanka during the second
quarter of the twentieth century as well as their complacent
belief that Donoughmore and Soulbury were sufficient to the
task.[39] In 1956, many of the premises on which the United
National Party had been built would collapse.

## The Revivalist Alternative

Senanayake's confidence in a policy of moderation and restraint
appears, then, to have had something to do with not being
alert to what was happening around him. As prime minister,
he once dismissed the suggestion that "Sinhala should be
made the official language and Buddhism the state religion"
by saying that many other matters confronting him were more
urgent.[40] In at least one respect, that assessment was critically
mistaken. Whatever the best way to cope with nationalist
sentiments, nothing in the early 1950s needed more urgent
attention than the growing force of ethnic nationalism.

S. W. R. D. Bandaranaike did not make that mistake. He
was by no means as insensitive to the insistent realities of
the period as were Senanayake and his immediate UNP
successors, Dudley Senanayake and John Kotelawala. Indeed,

Bandaranaike ingeniously turned those realities to his own advantage and in the process helped to determine the basic direction of Sri Lankan political life for some time to come.

## The Donoughmore Buddhist

Bandaranaike's background was not all that different from Senanayake's, and, here and there, some of his political instincts were similar. If anything, Bandaranaike's family was even more closely identified with the British. Not only was his father "proudly and ostentatiously Anglican,"[41] but he himself was named after a British governor. He attended some of the same schools as Senanayake and then did him one better by going on to university in England at Oxford. Had he measured up to his father's expectations, he would have taken his rightful place in the anglicized elite of Sri Lanka and fallen readily into step with Senanayake and his pro-British colleagues.

But Bandaranaike did not measure up, nor he did he care to. In family and other associations he marched to his own beat. From an early age he resisted parental direction, isolated himself in school and elsewhere, and nursed a feeling of superiority toward others, including the Senanayakes.[42] All this was done, as he pictured it, in the service of fulfilling his destiny, of vindicating his personal "greatness."[43]

At Oxford, Bandaranaike excelled as a debater and public speaker, using experiences of prejudice against non-English students like himself as an incentive to outshine his classmates. His crowning oratorical accomplishment, interestingly, came in a debate in 1922 in which he attacked continuing control over India as an offense against British political ideals. In Bandaranaike's eyes, achieving a reputation as one of the best orators at Oxford was the "final triumph" of his "lonely struggle" and a confirmation of his policy of self-reliance.[44]

Bandaranaike's rhetorical skills marked him as a promising politician as soon as he returned to Sri Lanka in 1925. His father wanted him to pursue a civil service career, but he favored the life of electoral politics. He affiliated early on with the Ceylon National Congress—the mainline political association of the time—but simultaneously, if not altogether consistently, began to chart an independent course.

To his father's chagrin, Bandaranaike turned his back on Anglicanism and set about learning Sinhala to communicate with the people. He expressed firm, though as yet unfocused, support for nationalism. He spoke of the growing spirit of reverence for "the geographical area one's people inhabit" and for "one's customs, institutions, language and religion" as "nothing but a noble ideal."[45] He soon took to wearing national dress. In 1933, he published a small book entitled *Spinning Wheel and Paddy* patterned after the Gandhian model for India and dedicated to restoring the ancient, simple Sinhala Buddhist way of life in Sri Lanka. About the same time, he converted to Buddhism, no doubt out of a mixture of personal conviction and political opportunism.[46]

Bandaranaike's Buddhism had a distinctly revivalist flavor. He had read many of Dharmapala's writings, had met the man himself on one occasion, and was especially influenced by a close political associate who was a follower of Dharmapala.[47] Bandaranaike espoused the same combination of personal discipline and social activism. Like Dharmapala, he "believed that Buddhism should be brought into the centre both of everyday life and of the political arena."[48] And at the height of his career in the late 1950s, Bandaranaike would be likened to Dharmapala's favorite Sinhala king, Duttagamani, and to the "strong vein of national emotionalism and romanticism" associated in the revivalist's mind with King Duttagamani.[49]

Whatever the personal motives for Bandaranaike's conversion, the political setting and consequences were also of great importance. In a word, the Donoughmore Constitution of 1931 was critical.[50] Its adoption created the conditions that encouraged Bandaranaike's "revivalist alternative." The pattern of de facto communal representation and of electoral domination by the Sinhala that followed from Donoughmore and universal suffrage, as well as the lack of incentives for ethnic cooperation, all led directly to the rise of communalism throughout Sri Lanka.[51] Communalism represented precisely what Bandaranaike had been waiting for: the opportunity to break loose from the dominance of the Senanayakes and the Ceylon National Congress and to build his own distinctive political organization loyal primarily to him.[52]

The first important manifestation of this new political movement was the founding in 1936 of the Sinhala Maha Sabha (the Great Sinhala League). A group of radical young Sinhala politicians and university and literary figures, including Dharmapala's protégé, Sirisena, were behind it, with Bandaranaike playing a central role.[53] Although he had flirted with a policy of pluralism and tolerance in the mid-1920s, by the mid-1930s Bandaranaike concluded that "nationalism based on cultural revival among the Sinhalese-speaking Buddhists was the only solution" to colonialism.[54] Accordingly, the central objective of the Sinhala Maha Sabha was to establish Buddhism and Sinhala culture as the foundation of Sri Lanka's identity.[55]

In 1939, as though to underscore the point, Bandaranaike publicly discussed the meaning of nationhood. If the heart of a nation is, as he suspected, "the people," he did not know, he said, of any country that "had progressed to the goal of freedom by embracing all communities and all cultures in their activities."[56] In the same year he told a gathering, "I am prepared to sacrifice my life for the sake of my community, the Sinhalese. If anybody were to hinder our progress, I am determined to see that he is taught a lesson he will never forget."[57] Although he would not have appreciated the reference, Bandaranaike was favorably compared, after the speech, to Hitler.[58]

Tamil reaction was predictable. Statements like Bandaranaike's, reflecting as they did the views of influential Sinhala politicians, "had the untoward effect of completely undermining the confidence of the Ceylon Tamil elite in the prospect of their culture being accepted on an equal footing with that of the Sinhala Buddhists."[59] After Bandaranaike delivered a "particularly fiery communalist speech about the 'glorious history of the Sinhalese'" to the Sinhala Maha Sabha, a Tamil colleague rebuked him: "Sinhalese history was a record of constant wars. They either killed each other or killed the Tamil invader. I do not know whether [Duttagamani] was a vegetarian or an anti-dowry philosopher like my honourable friend, but according to history, he did not practice [harmlessness] when it came to getting rid of King Elara."[60] By 1939, Tamil politicians were enunciating their own version of communalism, drawing on perceived connections with South India. "All of us Tamils owe allegiance to India, and are thankful to her for the spiritual gifts and privileges which she gave us. Our is a civilization and we, Dravidians, have a pre-Aryan culture. . . . We Tamils must preserve this Dravidian civilization. We have a past behind us of which we need not be afraid."[61]

## The Mobilization of the Monks

Bandaranaike's eventual political success was the result of his ability to harness the growing resentment and discontent among the Sinhala majority over the failure to achieve their national aspirations. The majority believed their culture and religion had been violated by a long line of colonial oppressors, particularly by the British, and they were enraged that the Tamils and other minorities might dare to obstruct the fulfillment of their historic destiny. Economic factors only intensified their rage. The fact that Tamils occupied a disproportionately large share of public sector employment compounded Sinhala frustration.

During the 1940s and early 1950s, a group of Buddhist monks became the advance guard of Sinhala frustration. Thus, "political bhikkhus," as they were called, came to play a major role in bringing about the triumph of ethnocracy in the election of 1956.[62]

As early as the 1930s, a small band of radical Sri Lankan monks broke away from the pattern of monastic withdrawal and social inactivity characteristic of the time and identified with the ideals of socialism and nationalism. One of the well-known leaders, Udakandeawela Siri Saranankara, acquired these ideas by associating with anticolonial movements in India, where he had gone, interestingly enough, as an acolyte of Anagarika Dharmapala.[63] He and his followers eventually joined various Sri Lankan Marxist and worker parties springing up at the time.

The radical monks were centered in the leading monastic college, Vidyalankara Pirivena, outside Colombo. They were part of a tradition of activism going back, in the early twentieth century, to the temperance movement and to working-class agitation that was partly inspired by Dharmapala and was further stimulated by the special ties with India that he fostered.[64] By 1946, the radical monks had gained stature and confidence. They issued the "pathbreaking" Vidyalankara Declaration, which is still the charter for radical monks today.[65]

The declaration's message is unequivocal: it proclaims "the right and responsibility of monks to participate in politics, in matters to do with the public weal, and in the nationalist movement and decolonialization process." It urges monks to postpone their own individual salvation and to band together into a political pressure group to achieve social improvement.[66]

The monks' first real show of strength came around the time of the election of 1947. To begin with, the Ceylon Union of Bhikkhus (LEBM) adopted several resolutions rejecting the Soulbury Constitution for failing to guarantee genuine national independence or a sufficiently nationalized economy. There was strong support for striking workers, and in the election, which the UNP won, monks were active in the campaigns of all the major parties, including the left-wing parties.[67]

Such activity was preparation for "the forceful and effective participation by monks"[68] in the election of 1956, participation that would mark "the zenith of Bhikkhu influence in the country."[69] In mid 1951, Bandaranaike left the UNP to found his own party, the Sri Lanka Freedom party (SLFP), as the direct successor to Sinhala Maha Sabha. "From the outset the new party offered a home to those who rejected the concepts of a polyethnic polity, of a Sri Lankan nationalism, and of a secular state."[70] Accordingly, "the radical monks found a party which was close to their concept of politics."[71]

They became very active on the side of the SLFP and as a matter of fact "were largely responsible for creating the [party's] identity as a 'Sinhala-Buddhist' party."[72] Indeed, "the election of 1956 was introduced in Buddhist terms by monks who were the chief speakers on SLFP platforms, as a 'Mara Yuddha,' a fight against evil."[73]

In becoming a force for religious and ethnic nationalism, the political bhikkhus were influenced by three important, politically charged texts published in the 1940s and 1950s: *The Heritage of the Bhikkhu* (1946), by a monk-scholar named Walpola Rahula; *The Revolt in the Temple* (1953), by D. C. Vijay-awardena, a Buddhist layman; and *The Betrayal of Buddhism* (1956), published by the Buddhist Committee of Inquiry.

In *The Heritage of the Bhikkhu*, Rahula attacks "the fallacy of Mr. Senanayake and his followers," who had "voiced the opinion that Buddhist monks should not participate in public affairs."[74] On the contrary, Buddhist monks, according to Rahula, are enjoined by their tradition to attend to matters of health, sanitation, righteous government, and the like. Beyond that, it is impossible to separate "nationalism" and "national culture" from "religion" in Sri Lankan history, so that terms like "religio-nationalism" and "religio-patriotism" are indispensable for capturing the spirit of Sri Lankan Buddhism. In the spirit of Dharmapala,

> Rahula marshalls examples to establish that time and again monks participated in the politics of the country—settling court and succession disputes, sometimes actively selecting a candidate and conferring kingship on him, and even marching to war as in the time of [Duttagamani]. 'Custodians of freedom' on every occasion of danger to both nation and religion, the monks came forward to save and protect them. This comment by Rahula [would] resonate well into the latter part of the twentieth century: *'The religio-patriotism at that time assumed such overpowering proportions that both bhikkhus and laymen considered that even killing people in order to liberate the religion and the country was not a heinous crime.'*[75]

Also in the spirit of Dharmapala, Rahula laments "the enervating and castrating effect of foreign, especially British, rule upon the *sangha* and the vocation and public position of the monk in society."[76] The British had actually conspired against Buddhism in Sri Lanka, he wrote. They had sought to weaken its hold in order to Christianize the country. In the short term, the policy worked. Monks lost their central place in society and with it the respect of the people. They retreated into their temples and performed marginal services. Rahula's book was intended to reverse that trend and to restore Buddhism to its central political role.

*The Revolt in the Temple* picked up on the nationalist theme, asserting that Sri Lanka "was primordially destined as a land that united Buddhism with the Sinhalese nation."[77] According to the author,

> Throughout their history, the stimulus to action, for the Sinhalese, was the ideology that they were a nation brought into being for the definite purpose of carrying, "for full five thousand years," the torch lit by the [Buddha] twenty-five centuries ago; and the structure of Sinhalese society has been shaped in pursuance of this ideology. Buddhism was the State Religion. The chosen king was always a Buddhist, and the people supported him with wholehearted loyalty, because he, as the chief citizen of the country, was the leader in shaping and sustaining their ideology, and the protector of the national faith. The temple became the centre from which radiated learning, arts, and culture. The Sangha were the guides of the king's conscience and the mentors of the people, whose joys they shared and whose sorrows they assuaged.[78]

*The Betrayal of Buddhism* was the report of the Buddhist Committee of Inquiry established in 1954 by the All Ceylon Buddhist Congress. The committee's task was to assess the state of Buddhism in Sri Lanka and to recommend ways of improving its position. The committee was composed of scholar monks and officials of monastic colleges along with a group of Buddhist laymen, including a disciple and protégé of Dharmapala. The special occasion for this investigation was the Buddha Jayanti, the twenty-five-hundredth anniversary of Buddha's achievement of final nirvana, to be celebrated in 1956, the same year as the fateful election for prime minister.

The report rehearsed the familiar revivalist themes. It recalled the sense of peril under which the Sinhala have long lived—the peril of Tamil invasion in ancient times; and the peril of colonial domination more recently. It harked back to the golden age of the Buddhist kings, such as Duttagamani and Parakramabahu I, and called for a restoration of past glories by compensating Buddhists for years of neglect caused by pro-Christian colonial policy. The report recommended setting up both a Buddhist council that would help to implement "all the prerogatives of the [ancient] Buddhist kings as regards the Buddhist religion" and a ministry for religious affairs aimed at rehabilitating those religions that "have suffered under colonial rule."[79]

The educational recommendations reflected deep antipathy toward the Christian missionary movement, and especially toward missionary schools. The report recommended withdrawing all grants in aid to Christian schools, and placing all schools forthwith under the control of the state, on the assumption that "government policy would favor the transmission of Buddhist values, Sinhalese language and literature, and 'traditional culture.'"[80] In a concluding chapter entitled "Tolerance," the report accused Buddhists of having been tolerant to a fault. Although they should continue to respect other religions, they nevertheless had a right to expect that Sinhala Buddhism would regain its old status.[81]

The desire to revive what was thought of as the ancient ethnic tradition—a desire reflected in these publications and intensified by the political bhikkhus—"became, in the messianic atmosphere of the Buddha Jayanti, the prime determinant of a process of change" aimed at extending Sinhala Buddhist political predominance throughout all of society.[82] This spirit found full expression in the election of Bandaranaike in 1956. The report of the Committee of Inquiry provided a platform on which Bandaranaike could run and could promote himself as the protector of Buddhism.[83] "It is no exaggeration to claim that the 1956 election . . . was the climactic and singular moment in twentieth-century political life, when a significant number of monks temporarily organized to win an election."[84]

*six*

# Full Circle

## "A Great Opportunity, Fatefully Missed"

In December 1992 the *Economist* reported: "Some forty years
after the idea was rejected, politicians in Sri Lanka are again
considering turning the country into a federation as a way
out of its civil war."[1] Remarkably, the current peace plan,
under which increased power and a degree of political and
cultural autonomy would devolve to the Tamils in the northern and eastern sections of the country, is very similar to an
arrangement sketched out in 1957 by Bandaranaike, soon after
his election as prime minister, and an eminent Tamil leader,
S. J. V. Chelvanayagam. As one observer recently stated, if
"the politicians had agreed to this in the 1950s, it would have
saved [the] country a lot of bloodshed."[2] Or, in Tambiah's
ringing words, this agreement was "a great opportunity,
fatefully missed, to settle the Tamil question for all time."[3]

The Bandaranaike-Chelvanayagam pact, as it was known,
was but the outline of a solution to ethnic strife in Sri Lanka.
But the pact contained the ingredients for what is increasingly
accepted as a basis for reasonable and peaceful accommodation.[4] As such, the agreement marked a moment of sanity
in a period of growing social derangement.

By implication, the pact acknowledged that Sri Lanka is a
multiethnic society. Tamil was to be recognized as "a national
language," and the northern and eastern provinces, where

around 70 percent of the Tamil population lives, were to be administered in the Tamil language, albeit with full protection for the non-Tamil minorities inhabiting the area. Regional councils were to be created to modify an overcentralized political system that appeared to favor the majority. Significantly, the regional councils would have the power of selecting homesteaders to be admitted into predominantly Tamil areas under government irrigation and land development programs.[5]

That Bandaranaike was disposed at all to compromise with the Tamils, having just been thrust into office in a surge of Sinhala chauvinism, indicates the depth of his awakening anxiety over the very revivalism he had up to that time so effectively exploited and encouraged.

He began to appreciate, for instance, that many of the bhikkhus who had supported him harbored utterly utopian expectations for the future of Sri Lanka and had acquired a greatly exaggerated sense of their own political importance. Even more worrying, they displayed a "hard-eyed, zealous intolerance" toward divergent points of view.[6] In contrast, Bandaranaike's convictions were much more politically motivated and subject to compromise. As events unfolded, it became clearer and clearer that revivalism for Bandaranaike was more a convenience than a cause.

At the same time, whatever Bandaranaike's reservations and however ready he might now be to take up a more pragmatic approach to ethnic tension, it would prove hard to contain the communalist and ethnocentric passions associated with revivalism once they had been unleashed.[7] Indeed, it was those very passions, which Bandaranaike himself helped to encourage, that eventually caused the demise of the Bandaranaike-Chelvanayagam pact and indirectly, at least, brought an end to Bandaranaike's administration and his life.

## The Language Problem

The way Bandaranaike handled the burning question of language during his administration illustrates his predicament.

Language, or what has been called "linguistic nationalism," was at the heart of Sri Lanka's ethnic problem.[8] In the election campaign, Bandaranaike rallied revivalist support by advocating the policy "Sinhala Only," according to which Sinhala would become the exclusive official language of Sri Lanka. For the ethnic nationalists, that point was essential. Sinhala culture and religion were deeply interconnected with the language,[9] and therefore the Sinhala way of life could achieve its rightful preeminence only if the Sinhala language predominated.

For the Tamils, this policy was profoundly offensive. It revoked a more flexible and pluralistic linguistic arrangement worked out in the early 1940s before independence,[10] and it appeared to devalue and demean the Tamils by subordinating their language. What is more, making Sinhala alone the official language was thought to legitimate a Sinhala Buddhist ideology embedded in the language, an ideology that implied, for example, that "loyalty to the country is identified with loyalty to a particular 'race' and religion—that of the majority."[11] Also by implication, the policy was interpreted as authorizing certain discriminatory and demeaning attitudes toward Tamils that "lie concealed in the very structures" of the Sinhala language.[12] Most urgently, the Tamils believed that the Sinhala Only policy would lead to enormous educational and economic disadvantages for them, especially regarding employment opportunities in the professions and government.[13]

In his conciliatory postelection mood, Bandaranaike strove to soften the impact of Sinhala Only, even though he had raised chauvinist expectations on the subject during the campaign. He now attempted to include in the relevant bill several mollifying provisions guaranteeing what he called a "reasonable use of Tamil." Eventually, he decided to withdraw the provisions under revivalist pressure, an act of acquiescence that worsened ethnic relations and provoked "the worst episode of communal violence in modern Ceylon's history to that time."[14]

Despite the setback, Bandaranaike continued to assure Tamil leaders that he would protect their interests in the matter.

After the new law took effect, Bandaranaike virtually nullified its effects by issuing a public statement that languages
other than Sinhala already in official use might so continue
until further notice.[15] Obviously, his agreement with Chelvanayagam that Tamil might be considered "a language of
Ceylon" and thus enjoy at least informal parity with Sinhala
was part of this new spirit of magnanimity.

However, the "language loyalists" among the Sinhala would
have none of it. For them, recognizing Tamil as an official
language of any sort violated the Sinhala Only Act and
undermined the whole idea of Sinhala supremacy. They
began to resist Bandaranaike's temporizing ways, demanding
that he remember who elected him and that he honor the
goals of revivalism. Accordingly, Bandaranaike's attempts to
defuse the language issue only inflamed and emboldened
the linguistic nationalists.

## The Revivalist Revenge

Nevertheless, Bandaranaike persisted. He continued to seek
ways to sweeten the pill for the Tamils. He drafted a regional
councils bill in July 1956, which would have given some
political autonomy to Tamil-majority areas, and he suggested
amendments to the constitution to protect minority rights.[16]
These proposals anticipated the terms of the Bandaranaike-
Chelvanayagam pact, which, considering the growth of
revivalist resentment at the time, was negotiated with no
little temerity.

The simple result of all these conciliatory gestures, including the pact with Chelvanayagam, was failure. As with the
question of language, Bandaranaike miscalculated the effects
of his policies and proposals, naively exaggerating his own
ability to mediate differences and control events.

The immediate reaction to the pact among the Sinhala was
intensely negative. Even moderates such as Dudley
Senanayake condemned it as "an act of treachery," which
would lead, intolerably, to the country's partition. J. R. Jayewardene, leader of the UNP and future president, called it

a "betrayal of the Sinhalese" and used the occasion as an opportunity for "out-chauvinizing" the Sri Lanka Freedom Party.[17] Bandaranaike labored energetically to salvage the pact, but he was soon overwhelmed by the forces of extremism. It was "precisely at this time that the Buddhist monk pressure groups, . . . in conjunction with their lay sponsors and allies, stepped up their protest against a surrender to Tamil demands."[18] A group of bhikkhus who conducted a highly publicized act of *satyagraha*, or civil disobedience, in front of Bandaranaike's house galvanized the revivalists and soon succeeded in forcing the prime minister to renounce completely the terms of the pact.

The Tamils in turn protested what they considered Bandaranaike's abject capitulation by resorting to a mass civil disobedience campaign of their own. There then followed another outbreak of interethnic violence—this one more severe, widespread, and destructive than the earlier incidents in 1956 and punctuated, significantly, with attacks against priests and temples in both communities.[19]

In the aftermath of the violence, Bandaranaike still attempted to ease the apprehensions of the Tamils. He cracked down on the Sinhala rioters and saw to it that a bill authorizing the use of Tamil was passed. Once again, the result was not what he hoped for. The activist bhikkhus, offended as they had been in the past at Bandaranaike's conciliatory spirit, retaliated by asserting their influence within the SLFP. They set about ridding the party of its leftist ministers, whose lack of sympathy for Sinhala revivalism was considered a bad influence on Bandaranaike. Their efforts produced severe dissension and fragmentation within the SLFP, which undoubtedly weakened the party's effectiveness and in the bargain besmirched their own reputation as upright followers of the Buddha. But they did at least prevent Bandaranaike from forfeiting revivalist objectives by compromising with the Tamils.[20]

However, the bhikkhus went even further. On September 25, 1959, one of them took Bandaranaike's life. The details were rather sordid. The assassin, himself a monk, was under the spell of another infamous and unscrupulous monk with illicit political and commercial interests, who nevertheless was highly influential in the SLFP. That Bandaranaike was killed by such people indicated just how far things had gone. Here were Buddhist bhikkhus, sworn to nonviolence and to a life set apart from worldly temptations, committing murder in pursuit of earthly prestige and wealth. But just as ironic, the very people who did Bandaranaike in were the sort of people he himself had cultivated, whose ideals of religious nationalism he had espoused, whose positions of political influence he had strengthened. He had set out expecting to make use of revivalism and then to tame it. He was not the first to have miscalculated. He would not be the last.

## The Advance of Ethnocracy

Sirimavo Bandaranaike, wife of the assassinated leader, replaced her husband immediately after his death and then was herself elected prime minister as the SLFP candidate in 1960. Not sharing her husband's ambivalence toward Sinhala revivalism, she promptly encouraged linguistic nationalism and Buddhist supremacy. She insisted that the full implications of the Sinhala Only Act be enforced. Sinhala would become the exclusive language of administration throughout the island by early 1961, and there would be no serious concessions to the Tamils, despite an agreement worked out during the 1960 election.[21]

### Buddhist-Christian Tensions

In addition, Mrs. Bandaranaike delighted revivalists by extending state control over education as a way of reducing Christian influence. In part, no doubt, because of their disproportionately large influence, especially in education, Roman Catholics became ready targets. The curricula and pattern of instruction of the highly prestigious Catholic schools were placed, accordingly, "at the mercy of the government."[22] Along with the whole school system, Christian schools were to be subjected to "increasing Buddhist influence," "both at the national and the grass-roots level."[23] They were suddenly faced with the unpalatable choice of acquiescing to state domination or forfeiting all state assistance. The Catholic minority concluded that they, like the Tamils, had become the victims of discrimination at the hands of the Sinhala majority. "They found that the constitution gave them no protection against the government on this issue. As long as a restriction was so devised that it was applicable [alike to all minorities] and not to a specific group, the constitutional obstacle [section 29(2) of the Soulbury Constitution, guaranteeing freedom from religious discrimination] could be [evaded]."[24]

Buddhist-Christian relations worsened. Disaffected military and police officers, themselves Christians, staged an unsuccessful coup d'état in 1962, which had the adverse effect of intensifying Buddhist chauvinism. One notable consequence was the elimination of Christians from both the military and the police, thereby ensuring that the enforcement of law and the administration of force would be in the hands of those who were "largely Sinhalese and Buddhist."[25]

To be sure, the bhikkhus, for their part, were now generally subdued, their reputation tainted by the unsavory circumstances surrounding a string of political excesses, including the assassination of the prime minister. Nevertheless, militant Buddhist laypeople filled in and helped to establish "the primacy of Buddhism and Buddhists in Sri Lanka's political system and public life" during Mrs. Bandaranaike's first term, which ended in 1965.[26] And nothing much changed in that respect in her second term, from 1970 to 1977.

Nor was revivalism's progress retarded during the intervening administration of Dudley Senanayake (UNP), despite his disposition toward moderation. That accommodating spirit led him to strike a new, if unheeded, agreement with Chelvanayagam.[27] A coalition of the SLFP and UNP in parliament defeated a modest attempt to ease Tamil apprehensions by devolving some power to district councils, and Buddhist militants prevented Senanayake from providing expected relief to the Roman Catholics. In fact, resentment deepened when Senanayake yielded to a Buddhist scheme for arranging holidays so that the Christian sabbath was abandoned completely.

## Anti-Tamil Feeling and the 1972 Constitution

If anything, Mrs. Bandaranaike's second term exhibited "a more virulent anti-Tamil strain" than had existed in the 1960s.[28] A revised system of entrance requirements and geographical quotas restricted the access of Tamil students to university education and thereby substantially reduced their opportunity for government employment.[29] "Nothing has caused more frustration and bitterness among Tamil youth than this, for they regarded it as an iniquitous system deliberately devised to place obstacles before them."[30] The effects were felt more acutely in some places than in others: "The impact of the district quota system [was] severest on the Jaffna students. The sense of injustice it generated in the Jaffna Tamil community has been quite intense and has probably had far-reaching effects in inciting the young generation to militant forms of protest."[31]

It must be remembered that these policies, perceived by the Tamils as so discriminatory, were strongly motivated not only by ethnocentric revivalism, but also by the resentment of the Sinhala toward what they regarded as a system of university admissions and government employment unfairly favorable to the Tamils. It is true that the disproportionately large Tamil share of university places and government jobs in the 1950s and after implied a need for some readjustment toward a more equitable and representative admission and employment pattern. The problem, it appears, was lack of discretion and sensitivity on the part of the government in accomplishing that goal. "By stepping in to force the pace of this inevitable development and doing so in an obviously discriminatory manner," the government "caused enormous harm to ethnic relations. . . . "[32] The government solution made matters worse, not only between the Sinhala and the Tamils, but also within and among other groups, including different segments of the Sinhala community itself:

> The political impact of the district quota system has been little short of disastrous. It has convinced many Sri Lankan Tamils that it was futile to expect equality of treatment with the Sinhalese majority. . . . It has kindled resentment against the Muslims in both Tamil and Low-country Sinhalese areas and rendered relations between the Kandyan and Low-country Sinhalese more fragile than before.[33]

Representative of the deteriorating ethnic relations at the time was the new constitution adopted in May 1972 to replace the Soulbury. The tradition of liberal democracy, guaranteeing equal respect for all, was there in form and, on the surface at least, somewhat enhanced. Unlike the Soulbury Constitution, the new constitution had a bill of rights, including religious freedom. Moreover, in giving pride of place to the majority and its religion, the constitution did not go so far as other Buddhist countries such as Burma. It is also true that after the constitution was adopted, the Roman Catholics were able to work out something of an accommodation with the Sinhala majority.[34] Nevertheless, taken as a whole, the document was "in many ways a symbolic assertion of nationalism," which "enshrined the expectations of the Sinhalese Buddhist nationalists without a single [serious] concession to the Tamil speaking minority."[35]

For one thing, its adoption was not the result of an inclusive, accommodating process. Opposition groups either dissented vehemently or, like the Tamil Federal party, walked out of the Constituent Assembly altogether. Tamil opposition focused especially on chapters II and III, which touched on the sensitive subjects of religion and language. Chapter III declared Sinhala the one official language, with the use of Tamil to be determined by statute. By classifying the use of Tamil as a statutory matter, rather than entrenching it as basic right, the constitution surrendered Tamil interests to the vagaries of communal politics, which was of course just what worried the Tamils. As to the issue of religion, chapter

II reads: "The Republic of Sri Lanka shall give to Buddhism the foremost place and accordingly it shall be the duty of the state to protect and foster Buddhism while assuring to all religions the rights granted by Section 18(1)(d)."

Two things concerned the Tamils about this provision. The first problem was that it gave official privileges to the majority religion and thereby encouraged cultural biases—as in schools and public rhetoric—that favored one group above others. Beyond that, such a provision was in danger of leading to more tangible forms of discrimination, such as preferential treatment in regard to public benefits and advantages.

The second problem concerned the status of the protections guaranteed under section 18(1)(d). In a word, everything assured in that section was effectively nullified by the open-ended restrictions enunciated in the clause that directly followed. The enumerated limitations are surprisingly broad. Standard issues such as "public safety," "public order," "national security," and the "protection of public health or morals" are mentioned as grounds for modifying or suspending ordinary rights and freedoms. But other things seldom considered permissible are also included: "the interests of national unity and integrity," "national economy," and, most unexpected of all, anything that "gives effect" to something called the "Principles of State Policy," as specified elsewhere.

The philosophy behind all this was the special combination of Sinhala nationalism and socialist doctrine that inspired Mrs. Bandaranaike's coalition party. In this view, rights are expendable. They are a western, bourgeois concept, convenient for certain purposes but to be cheerfully denied when they conflict with government policy.[36] Accordingly, there was fierce government resistance to a strong, independent judiciary that could protect rights by supervising and restraining executive action.[37]

### The Tamil Response

As a symbol of "the linguistic politics that had dominated Sri Lankan [life] since 1956,"[38] the 1972 constitution became the focus of growing estrangement between the Sinhala and the Tamils. After its adoption, "the traditional [Sri Lankan] Tamil leaders felt helpless." "Their normal protest tactic, non-violent civil disobedience, had clearly failed."[39] In reaction, a radically new form of Tamil political self-consciousness began to take shape.

The Tamil leaders formulated a six-point program, making it public just two days after the adoption of the constitution. They hoped it would become the basis for a new accommodation, one that would rectify, from their point of view, the deep deficiencies of the existing constitution. There should be, they said, parity between Sinhala and Tamil as official languages. All Indian Tamils who had been treated as stateless under the 1948 law should be granted citizenship. Sri Lanka should be a distinctly secular state, one guaranteeing the equality of all religions, with no special privileges for any group. A firmly entrenched constitutional assurance of equal freedom for all Sri Lankan citizens should be provided. The fifth point, addressing the Tamils themselves and their deep-seated Hindu prejudices, said caste untouchability should be abolished. Finally, the Sri Lankan government should be decentralized to allow greater opportunity for Tamil self-government.[40] As might be expected, none of this had much appeal for Mrs. Bandaranaike's administration. There would be no negotiation of these terms.

Government rejection simply intensified and consolidated the opposition. In an awakening "pan-Tamil" spirit, the leaders began to reach out to the long-forsaken Indian (or Estate) Tamils, exemplifying a readiness to think in less "orthodox," caste-bound terms about their fellow Tamils. They organized themselves into the Tamil United Liberation Front (TULF) and, in a formal resolution issued in May 1976, advocated openly and solemnly for the first time a separate Tamil state in Sri Lanka.

A poignant illustration of just how far things had degenerated was the role in this story of Tamil leader S. J. V. Chelvanayagam, Bandaranaike's erstwhile peacemaking partner of 1957. Eighteen years after his portentous agreement,

Chelvanayagam gained political advantage by effectively reconstituting himself as an uncompromising Tamil separatist. In keeping with the new spirit of the TULF, he turned away from his earlier commitment to a pluralistic solution for Sri Lanka's ethnic problem. Instead, he called for Tamil self-determination, for the right of "the Eelam Tamil Nation" to "exercise the sovereignty already vested in the Tamil people and become free."[41] In the circumstances, these were fighting words. Several of Chelvanayagam's TULF colleagues were soon to be charged with sedition for advocating a separate state.

Chelvanayagam's references to an already established "Eelam Tamil Nation," poised to reassert and recover its ancient claims to sovereignty, reflected the consolidation and mobilization of Tamil national consciousness during this period. That emerging consciousness took shape around the idea of a traditional homeland, particularly in the northern and eastern sections of the island, whose origins were believed to date "from the dawn of history."[42] These ideas recalled previous suggestions about Tamils being the "original inhabitants of this island" that were associated with the early stirrings of Tamil nationalism in the 1930s.[43]

## J. R. Jayewardene: Buddhist Nationalism in a New Mode

### The Dharmistha Society

The election of 1977 represented a stunning change in Sri Lankan politics. The party of the Bandaranaikes, the SLFP, more or less in charge since 1956, was decisively turned out and replaced by a reconstituted UNP under the leadership of Junius Richard Jayewardene. The UNP won 140 of 168 seats, riding to power on Jayewardene's promise to reshape and transform economic and social policy.[44] His capacity to fulfill that promise would be sorely tested.

Jayewardene thought of himself as a creative combination of the new and the old. In economic affairs, he fashioned himself after the prime minister of Singapore, Lee Kuan Yew, and hoped to replicate Singapore's astounding accomplishments in growth rates and industrialization. On the political side, Jayewardene endeavored to amalgamate traditional Sinhala themes with a revised version of constitutional democracy.

On a state visit to Washington in 1984, he described himself to President Reagan as Sri Lanka's 193rd head of state, going all the way back to Prince Vijaya. He thought of himself as "the inheritor of the Sri Lankan monarchy," making speeches that "sounded eerily similar to arguments Sri Lankan kings are known to have made."[45] He was thoroughly comfortable likening himself to the ancient Sinhala rulers, Duttagamani and Parakramabahu I, as well as to the famous Indian Buddhist king, Asoka. Though he expressed loyalty to the institutions of democracy,[46] his opponents wondered whether he might not secretly prefer a traditional monarchy.[47] Moreover, his ardent support for the new constitution of 1978, with its provisions for a strong executive and other Gaullist features, raised apprehensions about the inclinations of his government toward "benevolent authoritarianism" and the "politics of personality."[48]

After his election, Jayewardene's first public address was delivered from the Temple of the Tooth Relic in Kandy. He left no doubt about the significance of that location:

> When the country enjoyed freedom it is from here the kings addressed the people. Those who became Prime Ministers with your assistance spoke from here. . . . Seventy percent of our country are Buddhists. Therefore we shall lead our lives according to the sacred words of the Buddha. . . . The UNP government aims at building a new society on the foundation of the principles of Buddha *Dharma*. We have a duty to protect the Buddha *sasana* [49] and to pledge that every possible action would be taken to develop it. At the same time we expect to help the cause of other religions equally.[50]

Throughout the election campaign, he had described the state of righteousness he hoped to introduce as a *dharmistha* society. The term recalls Asoka, the Indian king of the second century B.C., and the Buddhist regime he is alleged to have instituted. On this model, the sangha and the king work hand in hand to implement Buddhism. By their teaching and probity, monks set an example for government officials, who in turn are an example to the people. As it happens, Asoka was particularly famous for creating tolerance among different faiths on the basis of Buddha's ideas.[51] Jayewardene's closing words appear to recall that achievement.

Still, there is some ambivalence in Jayewardene's use of Asokan ideals. On the one hand, invoking Asoka in contemporary Sri Lanka symbolized not so much the pattern of tolerance and mutual respect among different groups as "the rising force of Buddhism in national life."[52] Though Jayewardene's new constitution, like its predecessor, the constitution of 1972, does guarantee freedom for all religions (articles 10 and 14), it continues to preserve the special place of Buddhism as the nation's "foremost religion" (article 9), specifying it as the duty of the state "to protect and foster the Buddha *sasana*." For Jayewardene, the "sensibilities of minorities were less important in shaping this UNP position than the desire to keep government, as such, moral":[53]

> Buddhism enjoyed a growing measure of expressive hegemony in the Jayewardene years. Government officials frequently appeared as guests at Buddhist occasions, where they spoke of their government's commitment to the religion in a way never before heard from Hindu, Christian, or Muslim members of government. The Ministry of Cultural Affairs concerned itself with Sinhala and Buddhist culture, to the exclusion of minorities and minority religions. . . . The Jayewardene government was expressively Buddhist. It addressed its pronouncements to a public it assumed was Sinhala and Buddhist.[54]

Appropriations to the Department of Buddhist Affairs, which Jayewardene increased substantially, provided for "direct state support to favoured Buddhist monks," the publication of biographies of monks, and the support of monastic schools.[55]

Jayewardene found other ways to extend special privileges to the Buddhist community. From 1977 to 1987, his government made substantial funding available for restoring Buddhist temples and relic mounds in the Cultural Triangle, the area connecting the historic cities of Anuradhapura, Polonnaruwa, and Kandy.[56] Significantly, Jayewardene decided to bring the *Mahavamsa* up to date. Essentially "a Sinhala work, intended for Sinhala readers," the contemporary part of the *Mahavamsa* addressed the period from 1935 to 1977—the very years, as it appeared to the authors, in which "Buddhism reemerged in the national life and electoral politics."[57]

On the other hand, Jayewardene also set out to restrain and rechannel the Buddhist influence in Sri Lankan public life. He was appalled by the degree of direct political involvement the bhikkhus had achieved in the late 1950s during Bandaranaike's administration. Jayewardene believed that, like the unattached forest monks for whom he had special esteem, bhikkhus should stick to their apolitical calling; they should provide spiritual leadership and not become a substitute for government. The dharmistha society would be the product of individual moral responsibility. It could not be imposed by law. When a delegation of Buddhists suggested that Jayewardene make Sri Lanka an out-and-out Buddhist republic, he resisted.[58] "The Buddha," he said, "never for a moment thought it was possible to reform society through legislation. . . . He set an example to others of fair play in administration, not taking revenge on political opponents, ensuring freedom and liberty for all people."[59]

Jayewardene's emphasis here on voluntary initiative and responsibility in moral and spiritual affairs conformed to his general preference for free enterprise. He endeavored to substitute a liberalized, diversified economy for the centralized, government-regulated economy identified with the Bandaranaikes and the SLFP. At the same time, the tension between his liberal sentiments and his Gaullist disposition toward central control was mirrored in his conflicting attitudes toward the government's role in religion.

## The Colonization Controversy

Partly in accord with his emphasis on economic development, Jayewardene gave high priority to government-sponsored irrigation and colonization policies initiated by the British, which D. S. Senanayake and his successors had reformed and augmented in various ways.[60] The new administration devoted special attention to a project known as the Accelerated Mahaweli Program (AMP), which was supposed to implement in six years a thirty-year plan proposed earlier and intended to use the waters of the Mahaweli River for generating electrical power and for developing the arid plains, known as the Dry Zone, north and east of the central highlands. Nearly 150,000 families were expected to be accommodated eventually in the newly fertile area.[61]

The AMP, like earlier colonization schemes, had led to severe controversy, both ethnic and scholarly. At bottom, disagreement surrounds the question whether government efforts to resettle people on land improved by irrigation programs are aimed primarily at expanding Sinhala lebensraum (and are thus calculated expressions of Sinhala Buddhist chauvinism) or reflect a consistent government concern about improving the lot of all Sri Lankans—Sinhala and Tamil alike. Generally speaking, the Tamil community has favored the first interpretation, and the Sinhala community the second. Scholars of the subject are similarly divided.[62] Above all, the subject must be treated with the utmost caution.

There are some points of agreement. As a result of policies such as the AMP there clearly has been a substantial transfer of Sinhala population, especially into the eastern section of the country, which many Tamils consider an important part of their traditional area of residence.

Nor is there any doubt that many Tamil leaders have viewed this expansion with suspicion and have typically expressed apprehension and resistance toward it. In 1976, the Vaddukodai Resolution charged that the Sinhala majority had violated the rights of the Tamil community by means of "a system of planned and state-aided colonization" and "recently encouraged Sinhalese encroachments calculated to make the Tamils a minority in their own homeland."[63] The last point about feeling a loss of political power and economic security seems especially important:[64] "The main objection to colonization has come because colonization is perceived as a weapon to change Tamil majority areas into Tamil minority areas."[65]

The debate is over the actual effects of and motives for these policies. On the one hand, a case is made, in keeping with typical Tamil perceptions, that the favorable share of land consistently allotted to Sinhala settlers proves that the government's policies are both discriminatory and inspired by Buddhist chauvinism. According to this view, the Sinhala have

> equated the colonization of the Dry Zone with a restoration of the greatness of the ancient Sinhalese Buddhist kingdom. The UNP consciously evoked the image of an idyllic Buddhist past in which Dry Zone irrigation provided the resources for a prosperous and cultured civilization. Officials of the Mahaweli Program appealed directly to this mythical past, in which Tamil Hindu invaders were hated enemies, to mobilize Buddhist support.[66]

However, it is retorted that most of the areas in which a majority of Sinhala are resettled were originally either uninhabited or not predominantly Tamil, or else were allotted in proportion to the populations of the various ethnic groups that make up Sri Lanka, an arrangement that even some Tamil leaders have found fair.[67] Some observers also contend that—at least until 1981 or so—population trends in the northern and eastern provinces did not support fears that Tamils were being reduced to a minority within their own territorial base.[68]

Fundamental to this side of the argument is the desire to discredit the idea of "a traditional Tamil homeland," supposedly in existence since the dawn of history. Since the middle 1970s, Tamil leaders had made much of this idea and had taken it to certify special Tamil claims to the northern

and eastern sections of the country. The counterargument is
that since, by hypothesis, no such historical warrant exists,[69]
the government, in allotting land as it has done, is not
necessarily violating legitimate Tamil interests and therefore
is not guilty of intentionally discriminating against Tamils
in the name of chauvinist objectives.[70]

There is the additional argument that far from trying to
favor one group or section of the country over another, the
government actually conceived of the irrigation and colonization schemes, including the AMP, in inclusive, inter-
dependent terms and therefore as a benefit to the whole
country. Water resources, emanating from one section of the
country—the predominantly Sinhala highlands—were part
of a wider ecosystem[71] and therefore should be shared, for
mutual benefit, with the northern and eastern provinces,
where the majority of Tamils live. In fact, the UNP was
criticized for irrigating and developing predominantly Tamil
areas rather than attending to the northwest part of the
island, where mostly Sinhala live.[72] In its defense, the government held that including essentially Tamil areas in the
benefits of land development would work as "an integrative
force," thereby "strengthening regional ties" between the
Sinhala and the Tamils.[73]

In further support of this line of argument is the assertion
that, in fact, the "selection of Projects for the AMP was based
largely on economic considerations" such as, first and foremost, "the need to increase as rapidly as possible Sri Lanka's
power generating capacity."[74]

It seems probable that each side of this controversy possesses some part of the truth in what is undoubtedly a highly
complicated issue. While population changes in the contested
areas may not have been as ominous before 1981 as has been
alleged, there is evidence of significant alteration more
recently, alteration with serious implications, apparently, for
both the Sinhala and the Tamil communities.

> [Post-1981] developments ... have aroused deep concern on
> both sides. In the Northern districts there has been an influx of

Indian Tamils from the plantations who have encroached extensively on State lands and established illegal settlements. The
Sinhalese regard this as part of the separatist strategy. In the
East there have been large-scale encroachments by Sinhalese on
lands which are to be developed under the Mahaweli Scheme,
as well as in other areas in which Tamils or Muslims are in the
majority. These are seen by the Tamil community as attempts
to establish a strong Sinhala presence in the predominantly
Tamil-speaking areas.[75]

No doubt, illegal squatting by the Indian Tamils on state
lands in the northern districts intensifies tensions associated
with the colonization schemes. On the other hand, there is
widespread concern that one of the deep deficiencies of the
government programs has been the systematic failure to
include the Indian Tamils in the benefits of land distribution
and other welfare measures.[76]

Also, there seems some consensus, despite the understandable sensitivity of the issue, that the government
should acknowledge that "the transfer of Sinhala settlers
to the Tamil areas on a scale which significantly diminishes
the role and position" of the Tamils who have by now
firmly established themselves there is "not equitable."[77] It
is inequitable not because transfers violate rights to some
pristine "historic homeland" but because, in the present
context, they undermine a rightful sense of political and
economic security on the part of the Tamils and thus further alienate the Tamils from the Sri Lankan government.[78]
A policy that reaffirms and accounts for that principle, as
well as enforcing it, appears to be indicated. Admittedly,
there remains room for considerable disagreement over
applying the principle. Still, a general declaration of that
sort would provide official reassurance to an apprehensive
minority and perhaps more readily smooth the way to an
eventual resolution of the conflict. It is worth recalling that
both the Bandaranaike-Chelvanayagam pact of 1957 and
the Senanayake-Chelvanayagam pact of 1965 went to some
lengths to affirm and protect Tamil interests with respect
to colonization.

It is evidently important, before attributing blame, to identify and give proper emphasis to all aspects of the government's intentions and objectives in carrying out development
schemes such as the AMP.[79] At the same time, it is hard to
deny that the Jayewardene administration itself did make
something of the "golden threads" that were supposed to
connect contemporary irrigation and colonization projects
with those of ancient Sinhala kings. It talked fairly freely of
the need to restore the ancient achievements "to their former
glory."[80] Even if such words were only rhetorical,[81] they
distracted attention from objectives that were plausibly more
important—namely, economic development for the common
good. In justifying its irrigation policies, it is likely the
government could have contributed to improved ethnic
relations by concentrating on economic development and
by disregarding altogether inflammatory references to past
Sinhala glory.[82]

### The Failure of the Minorities Policy

Partly because the UNP had attracted some support from the
minorities in the election of 1977, partly because of an awareness that economic development depends on domestic stability and harmony, and partly, perhaps, because of his loyalty
to the Asokan ideal of tolerance, Jayewardene came to office
promising a new policy of conciliation toward the Tamils.
    However ambiguous the new constitution might be regard-
ing religion, it significantly upgraded the status of the Tamil
language, and it instituted a system of proportional representation for parliamentary and presidential elections, which
could possibly give greater weight to the Tamil vote.[83]
Changes in the university admissions policy made things
more equitable for the Tamils. Finally, district development
councils were created as an important step toward decentralization of authority and, consequently, toward a larger
measure of Tamil autonomy.[84]
    However, the policy of reconciliation did not work. For one
thing, the "possibility of improved ethnic relations was . . .

undermined by the government's failure to implement its policies wholeheartedly."[85] The district development councils possessed less authority than advertised, and their effectiveness was marred by budget cuts and other political distractions.[86] The bureaucracy frustrated attempts to broaden the official use of Tamil in accord with constitutional requirements,[87] and despite Jayewardene's emphasis on rectitude and probity in government, his administration was widely accused of dissipating its energies in fraud and favoritism.

For another, some Tamil groups were by now thoroughly committed to violence, believing the concessions contained in the 1978 constitution to be too little and too late. Violent, if localized, conflict erupted in the summer of 1977, and again in 1981, and contributed to a growing sense of peril in the Sinhala community. The stringent emergency measures adopted by the Jayewardene government in hope of containing the burgeoning civil war only served to increase tensions.

The first measure was the Prevention of Terrorism Act (PTA), adopted in 1979, an instrument of restraint that itself became a cause of further embitterment. Its provisions and powers were unusually broad.[88] One of Jayewardene's more extreme ministers urged relaxing the law on grounds of the extraordinary circumstances Sri Lanka found itself in: "Terrorism cannot be stopped, and never has been stopped by means of law. Terrorism has been stopped by terrorism. . . . Terrorists are like dogs."[89]

The act (which is still in force) gave the government considerable extrajudicial discretion in arresting and detaining persons suspected of terrorism. For all practical purposes the legislation might be applied retroactively.[90] It relaxed restraints against official torture by placing the burden of proof on the defendant to show that evidence obtained in custody was not the result of cruel or inhuman treatment.[91] Particularly sensitive was the prohibition against speaking or writing words or giving signs intended to cause "religious, racial or communal disharmony or feelings of ill-will or hostility between different communities or racial or religious groups."[92] Accordingly, the act might be invoked against utterances the government regarded as inflammatory, such as advocacy of a separate state for the Tamils or allegations of discrimination against the Tamils.

The PTA provided the warrant for an aggressive campaign by the government against the Tamil stronghold in the northern province, a campaign that produced large-scale arrests and detentions and used controversial military operations and forms of interrogation. By 1981 Tamil terrorism in the north had intensified and "provoked the security forces into committing atrocities in return." Anti-Tamil riots erupted in the fall after the funeral of a Sinhala policeman killed in a terrorist attack, revealing "an increasingly fearful mood among many Sinhala, who felt that their country was being dismembered by Tamil terrorists."[93]

Order began to disintegrate in 1982 after Jayewardene won a second term and decided to try to extend parliament's term of office for six more years. He succeeded, but only over persistent charges of fraud, intimidation, and patronage. Worst of all, the stage was set for "the horrific riots of 1983."[94] The causes lay "in the fear of Tamil terrorism, the belief that the country's problems could be solved if only 'the Tamils could be put in their place,' and the institutionalization of political violence by the major political parties."[95] In response to the funeral of several Sinhala soldiers killed in the north, mob violence broke out and quickly spread beyond the capital city of Colombo, where the funerals were held. The riots caused substantial harm to the Tamil community, including widespread injury, property damage, perhaps several thousand dead, and many thousands of Tamils in refugee camps. Law and order broke down altogether, with the security forces condoning, and in places inciting, the anti-Tamil violence.

Tamils in greater and greater numbers came to perceive the government as the enemy and began providing support for Tamil guerrilla groups in the northern and eastern parts of the country. As they saw it, not only was there no protection against Sinhala mobs or against the government's own excesses, but the government had responded to

the plight of the Tamils with almost total indifference. "After
the 1983 [riots], . . . a prominent minister spoke to the nation
of the hardship faced by the Sinhala, now forced to queue
up for food. He said nothing of, or to, the 70,000 Tamils in
refugee camps."[96] President Jayewardene himself did not
comment on the riots until five days after they began.
Finally appearing on television, he expressed no sympathy
for the Tamil victims but observed only that the Sinhala
people had reacted to "this violence by the [Tamil] terrorists." It was high time, he said, "to accede to the clamour
and the national respect of the Sinhala people" and to outlaw further talk and agitation for division and separatism.[97]
Nor was any effort made to bring to justice those in the
security forces who during the riots had been derelict in
their duty.

President Jayewardene's response was part of a wider
belief within the government and among the Sinhala majority
that the ultimate justification for anti-Tamil violence rested
on "the assertion of a Sinhalese identity which incorporates
inherent 'natural' rights to political ascendancy in an undi-
vided island."[98] The argument was frequently heard among
people on the streets and "was also made explicit in various
speeches broadcast to the nation by Cabinet ministers
[besides the president] throughout this period."[99]

> Implicit in all [these] statements is the fundamental premise
> that Sri Lanka is inherently and rightfully a Sinhalese state; and
> that this is, and must be accepted as, a fact and not a matter of
> opinion to be debated. For attempting to challenge this prem-
> ise, Tamils have brought the wrath of the Sinhalese on their
> own heads; they have themselves to blame.[100]

Matters deteriorated even further with the imposition of
several more pieces of legislation that were intended to mol-
lify the conflict but, instead, appeared to intensify it. The
first was a set of new emergency regulations adopted by the
parliament in mid-1983, including the infamous (and later
repealed) Regulation 15A, which permitted the security forces
to dispose of bodies secretly. Critics argued that such

permission "could open the way to the worst kind of extra-judicial execution."[101]

A second measure was also adopted in 1983. It was the sixth amendment to the constitution, which incorporated Regulation 15A and implemented President Jayewardene's promise to outlaw separatist agitation. The amendment prohibited any citizen "directly or indirectly, in or outside Sri Lanka," from supporting, espousing, promoting, financing, encouraging, or advocating "the establishment of a separate State within the territory of Sri Lanka."[102] Even the peaceful advocacy of schemes for restructuring Sri Lanka was punishable.

By extension, all members of parliament were required to take a loyalty oath to an indivisible Sri Lanka. This the members of the TULF, the moderate political wing of the Tamil community, refused to do, and they thereby lost most of their remaining political influence. Tamil confidence in the established political system declined accordingly.

As a result, Tamil guerrilla activity increased, and the government lost control of the Jaffna peninsula in the north. Capitalizing on the long-standing sense of identity between the Sri Lankan Tamils and the Tamil Nadu section of South India, the guerrillas received support from the Indian security service and took sanctuary in South India. In part by violently suppressing competing groups, the Liberation Tigers of Tamil Eelam (LTTE) gradually emerged as the dominant guerrilla force and began coordinating successful attacks against army outposts and Sinhala civilians, provoking a brutal cycle of violence and counterviolence. "The government security services responded to Tamil attacks by killing Tamils, often at random. Both sides committed terrible atrocities; torture and murder were common."[103]

## The Indo–Sri Lankan Agreement

Early in 1987, the government undertook to reassert control over the Jaffna peninsula in the face of growing Indian dissatisfaction with the way the Tamil problem was being handled. Increasingly attentive to the situation in Sri Lanka, the Indians took offense at the prospect of a bloody campaign against the Tamils and an eventual military occupation of the north by Sri Lankan forces, and they attempted to restrain that policy. The Indian prime minister, Rajiv Gandhi, thereafter succeeded in pressuring President Jayewardene into accepting the Indo–Sri Lankan Agreement to Establish Peace and Normalcy in Sri Lanka. The agreement was signed on July 29, 1987.

The agreement afforded some concessions to the Tamils. It acknowledged that "Sri Lanka is a multi-ethnic and multi-lingual plural society," and that "each ethnic group has a distinct cultural and linguistic identity which has to be carefully nurtured," and it urged preserving Sri Lanka's "character as a multi-ethnic, multi-lingual, multi-religious plural society, in which all citizens can live in equality, safety and harmony." While it declared that the "official language of Sri Lanka shall be Sinhala," it further declared that "Tamil and English will also be official languages."

The agreement envisioned a scheme for devolving administrative power to the northern and eastern provinces, where the majority of Tamils live. Specifically, it called for the temporary union of the two provinces "to form one administrative unit," thereby providing an expanded opportunity for self-government. A year later, the inhabitants of the eastern province, where the Sinhala and Muslims form a majority, might (at the discretion of the president) decide in a referendum "should remain linked with the Northern Province" or whether they should "constitute a separate administrative unit." In addition, the agreement called for a cease-fire, the disarming of Tamil guerrillas, and the dispatching of an Indian peacekeeping force to the northern and eastern sections of the country.

Initially, the Tamils cheered the proposals contained in the Indo–Sri Lanka Agreement, and the future brightened. A chance for peace and a new beginning appeared to be at hand. To be sure, the Sinhala were not of the same mind. There were mass demonstrations against the agreement encouraged by a militant Buddhist group, the Movement for

Protecting the Motherland (MSV: Mavbima Surakime Vyaparaya),[104] and by the Janatha Vimukthi Peramuna (JVP). Opponents saw the scheme as making the Tamils into a privileged minority and pushing the country closer to a dreaded partition. However, the government put the demonstrations down swiftly and effectively, and the Buddhist clergy were in some confusion over their response to the agreement, thereby diluting the opposition.

Nevertheless, the agreement did not hold. On the contrary, it increased violence. More and more Sinhala, even among the leadership in Jayewardene's own party, came to regard India's role as a dangerous threat to Sri Lankan sovereignty.[105] The JVP, outlawed since 1983, was emboldened by popular discontent, and conducted a campaign of terror against members of the UNP, as well as against members of the SLFP and some left-wing politicians who supported the agreement. Eventually, human rights activists, journalists, government managers, and prominent businessmen sympathetic to the agreement were all targeted. The JVP campaign, in turn, inspired retaliation by pro-government death squads allegedly connected to the police and military. There were increasingly indiscriminate attacks on the families and friends of those associated with either side, and by late 1989 deaths were running at about three hundred per week.[106]

Equally ominous, the LTTE, who had not acquiesced in the first place, soon took up arms against the agreement. Among other things, they did not favor giving the eastern province a chance to opt out of the devolution scheme, and they began punishing groups of Muslim, who rejected union with the Hindu Tamils in the northern province. In addition, the LTTE initiated several attacks against both the Indians and the Sinhala, and in October the IPKF retaliated. The fighting between the IPKF and the LTTE in the Jaffna area was extremely bloody. Many civilians were harmed, and it was claimed that the IPKF performed without due restraint. As a consequence, Tamil support for Indian intervention declined.

## The Movement for Protecting the Motherland

Despite Jayewardene's favorable attitude toward Sri Lanka's Buddhist heritage and his attempts to establish positive relations with the sangha, the UNP did not succeed in attracting strong support from the bhikkhus. "Buddhist monks were never comfortable with J. R. Jayewardene who had his own vision of Buddhism drawn from a textual interpretation of the canon. He emphasized canonical concepts and downgraded the ritual and social role of monks. His was an intellectual Buddhism."[107]

For one thing, Jayewardene's loyalty to the Sinhala cause was in doubt. In the 1977 election, the UNP had drawn votes from the minorities and from the Roman Catholic Church, and a part, at least, of the Catholic Church[108] was feared to be sympathetic to the Tamils.[109] For another thing, many monks worried about Jayewardene's "free market" and "consumerist" economic policies. The obsession with getting and spending, with attracting foreign investment and, concomitantly, with all the disreputable trappings of international capitalism threatened the modest life-style appropriate to Buddhism. In particular, newly available, superficial cultural products in literature, music, and the cinema would provide a severe challenge to traditional Buddhist teaching and practice. Perhaps most important, certain groups of monks, though by no means all,[110] strongly opposed the Indo–Sri Lankan Agreement and Indian intervention in Sri Lankan affairs.

All of these factors conspired to produce "the rapid politicization of the sangha" in the 1980s.[111] In July 1986, some radical monks formed the MSV, a loose collection of lay and clerical Buddhist organizations.[112] Some members of the MSV went on to ally themselves with the JVP in its violent campaign against the accord and the Jayewardene government.

The JVP and the MSV shared a natural affinity. Both groups were largely composed of rural Sinhala youth, captivated by an "equalitarian, 'Sinhala Buddhist' ideology." This ideology was combined with fervent appeals against militant Tamils, who were perceived as posing a severe threat to the "unity" and "sovereignty" of Sri Lanka. According to these groups, in seeking to divide the country either by creating a separate state or by devolving power in some new federal arrangement (as adumbrated in the Indo–Sri Lankan Agreement), militant Tamils and their sympathizers are nothing but "savages" of the sort who resisted the advent of Sinhala Buddhism when the country was founded in ancient times.[113] It is the Tamil extremists, not the Sinhala, who are "racist," since it is the Tamils who seek to partition the country according to race.[114]

The connection between the JVP and the militant monks had important implications.

> Unlike senior monks who still recognized the need for both self-realization and the discharging [of] social responsibilities, JVP monks place a premium on their political role. The JVP sangha organization was the first grouping of monks to participate in a May Day parade. About a thousand young monks clad in their distinctive saffron red robes walked under the banner of the Socialist Bhikkhu Front. Recognizing their special role, monks were positioned in the parade, immediately behind the JVP leadership. Later monks participated "en masse" in all JVP sponsored demonstrations.[115]

The JVP's advocacy of violence posed an obvious dilemma for Buddhist monks. Nevertheless, their tradition provided a solution. The notion, embedded in the chronicles, that the Sinhala are the proper custodians of Buddhism, that they are obligated to do what is required to protect the sangha and Buddhist teachings, "is so strong that monks are willing to rationalize the use of violence against the 'other,' even though it contravenes the basic tenets of Buddhism."[116] The arguments and strategies of realpolitik,[117] with the demand to do what is necessary in the name of Buddhism's survival, are at work here—arguments and strategies reminiscent of the exploits and achievements of King Duttagamani and the other heroes of Sinhala history.

The phenomenon of the radical political bhikkhu, evident during the Jayewardene years, is not, of course, representative of the total life and influence of Sinhala Buddhist monks. "The sangha has never acted as a unified monolithic agent; all shades of political preferences are reflected in its ranks."[118] To be sure, there is evidence that partly because of the underprivileged rural background out of which many of the younger monks come, a significant number continue to "perceive themselves as a deprived, alienated group inadequately recognized by both political authorities and the Buddhist public."[119] Insofar as that sense of frustration motivates certain monks to take up the cause of violent chauvinism, as has been the case with some members of the MSV, these monks obviously will continue to be part of the problem. Still, there are some countervailing indications as well, indications that may give greater promise of a positive contribution by some of the bhikkhus to resolving the ethnic conflict in Sri Lanka.[120]

In December 1988, Ranasinghe Premadasa, Jayewardene's prime minister, was elected president. Against the advice of his advisers and the SLFP, he immediately released several hundred JVP members as an initial show of good faith, but to no avail. In the midst of a degenerating situation, Premadasa urged the Indians to withdraw and then undertook an aggressive campaign designed to defeat the JVP, assisted, intentionally or not, by the pro-government death squads that had become so active in the wake of the discontent over the Indo–Sri Lankan Agreement. He accomplished both of his objectives. The IPKF completed its withdrawal by March 31, 1990, and by the end of 1989, most of the JVP leadership had been captured or killed. Indeed, it is probable that by inducing the Indians to leave, Premadasa succeeded at the same time in removing the major source of support among the Sinhala for the JVP.

## The Prospects for Peace

Even though the flurry of optimism over the prospects for peace evident at the end of 1992 appears to be losing power, there is still widespread agreement that, if they ever can be

implemented, the conditions for a lasting and equitable peace
in Sri Lanka are essentially elaborations of the Bandaranaike-
Chelvanayagam pact of 1957. Clearly, that is true of the parts
of the Indo–Sri Lankan Agreement that provided, for the long
term, "a basic framework for a settlement."[121] In the spirit of
the 1957 agreement, the accord "recognized the legitimacy of
the Tamil concerns. It made provision for language rights and
devolution. It formally established the principle that Sri Lanka
is a multiethnic society."[122]

By incorporating a countrywide system of provincial councils, the thirteenth amendment to the constitution entrenched
several of the elements sketched in the 1957 pact and elaborated in the Indo–Sri Lankan Agreement. The amendment
embraced the idea of the devolution of power, by which the
Tamil sections of the country as well as other regions could
be given substantial local control. It raised Tamil to the status
of an official language, along with Sinhalese, and also gave
English a special place. In turn, the sixteenth amendment
later "clarified and consolidated" these expansive language
provisions.[123] At least on paper, some of the important terms
for peace appear now to be in place.

Also, changing circumstances in the Sri Lankan civil war
suggest to some observers that the chances for implementing
these terms have improved lately.[124] The leader of the LTTE,
Velupillai Prabakharan, in response to a peace mission in
early 1993 by a Sri Lankan clergyman, announced he would
consider a solution well short of the standard demand for
an independent Tamil state,[125] and he has reiterated more
recently his willingness to enter into talks with the government
that could consider federation rather than separation.[126]

While Prabakharan's past record may not inspire confidence in his pledges, there is objective evidence that the
LTTE is now considerably weaker than it once was and
therefore, that it may need to contemplate new, less absolute
options. The Sri Lankan army has successfully driven the
insurgent forces from towns and villages in the eastern
province, including the coastal city of Batticaloa, enabling
the government to reassert control in the area. International

support, particularly that which emanated for so long from Tamil Nadu, has almost disappeared. The experience of the Indian army in Sri Lanka in the late 1980s fighting the LTTE; the assassination of Rajiv Gandhi in 1991, presumably at the hands of Sri Lankan Tamil militants; and the growing force of communalism in India have transformed the attitude of the Indian government toward the Tamil cause from sympathy and support to active hostility.[127]

Furthermore, the LTTE stronghold in the northern city of Jaffna, although still secure enough against the Sri Lankan army, "has been so heavily under siege that it has turned into a totalitarian pre-modern society, without electricity, running water, sewers or permitted dissent."[128] These conditions, together with the reputation of the LTTE for brutality, have strengthened resentment in the Tamil community at large toward the LTTE and have apparently encouraged expressions of greater moderation by certain Tamil leaders.[129] Finally, for many reasons, including the growing cost of the war,[130] the Premadasa government, before his assassination, seemed eager to take advantage of the improved military situation by "moving gradually toward talks with the Tigers."[131]

On the other hand, major obstacles remain. Whatever Prabakharan's recent utterances, and however badly his insurgents may be hurting, the LTTE has developed over the years certain vested interests, both political and financial, in continuing the civil war, and at least in most of the northern province, they are still able to enforce their will and to hold out against the army. In reality, compromise with the government may not, now and in the near future, be at all in line with the governing interests of the LTTE.

There are also the infuriating complexities and points of deep contention associated with implementing devolution. All seven Tamil political parties have regularly stated that there can be no satisfactory arrangement without a permanent merger of the northern and eastern provinces.[132] The Sinhala, and the Muslim minority living in the eastern province, resist this demand. They worry that the Tamil majority would abuse and suppress the Muslim and Sinhala minorities residing under their care, and there is, in fact, evidence that the LTTE has already displaced and otherwise mistreated minority inhabitants in the region.

One compromise proposes subdividing the populations into smaller units along the lines of the old district council model, but the Tamils reject this idea as causing "a fracturing of the Tamil polity."[133] A second compromise suggests redrawing the boundaries of the northern and eastern sections so that they will contain only Tamil Hindu citizens, leaving the Sinhala and Muslim minorities to work out their own political affiliation independently. Apart from the objection that such an arrangement would violate the "traditional homeland" of the Tamils, it is also claimed that the new divisions would artificially disrupt established living patterns and important social and cultural relations among different groups in the area. Furthermore, the exclusive concentration of Tamils in one area would give "the impression [that] the rest of Sri Lanka . . . is not a place where Tamils should live"[134] and, presumably, that non-Tamils have no place whatsoever in the area reserved for Tamils. This pattern of extreme segregation would not, it is contended, do much for developing the patterns of mutuality and tolerance that are basic to building a pluralistic, multiethnic society.

On May 1, 1993, President Premadasa was assassinated, apparently by the LTTE. Before that, his efforts at making peace had been weakened by impeachment efforts from within his own party and by a possible threat to his political future represented by a splinter group, the Democratic United National Front. In the wake of the political disruption caused by Premadasa's death, as well as continuing dissension within the UNP, it seems unlikely that there will be a breakthrough in peacemaking before the next presidential election in 1994.

But however uncertain the short-term prospects, the long-term achievement of peace in Sri Lanka undoubtedly depends on building an explicitly pluralistic, multiethnic political culture. That will require constructing political, legal, educational, and cultural institutions that enrich and expand on what might be called the basic terms of ethnic tolerance outlined in the Bandaranaike-Chelvanayagam pact thirty-six years ago and reaffirmed and clarified in the Indo–Sri Lankan Agreement and the thirteenth and sixteenth amendments.

The implications for "new thinking" may be fairly radical. For instance, it has been suggested that Sri Lankans need seriously to reexamine their constitution, particularly two of its central aspects: the unitary state and the presidential system.

> Both features have contributed toward a concentration of political authority in the president, and frustrated the promise made in 1987 of political devolution to Tamil-majority areas. The challenge is how to grant maximum autonomy to the Tamils without endangering the stability of the political system, which has hitherto espoused the majoritarian principle.[135]

Two distinct groups are at present agitating for constitutional reform in Sri Lanka. The northern rebels "want to dismantle the unitary state and ensure arrangements are made to share power." The "parliamentary rebels" in the south "are pressing for the abolition or reform of the presidential system to secure political freedoms and democratic accountability. They further contend that there can be no devolution when power is concentrated in the hands of a single individual."[136]

> The very definition of the state must change in Sri Lanka in order to reflect the ethnic diversity of the polity and to protect the rights of the Tamil and Muslim minorities. . . . The resolution of Sri Lanka's national question requires a democratic framework which accords primacy to civil and political rights and pluralistic values. Ethnic group rights are better secured in an environment in which there is a great respect for civil and political rights of the individual.[137]

It is argued, supplementarily, that ensuring the fundamental and equal rights of all citizens depends on a powerful judiciary.[138] This lack of a strong independent judiciary—and therefore the absence of sufficient provision for governmental accountability and rigorous protection of rights—appears to be the legacy of "Westminster consciousness" and the doctrine of parliamentary supremacy that so influenced the early stages of Sri Lanka's postcolonial experience.[139]

> The first chapter of the Constitution itself places the judiciary as a derivative body of parliament and therefore reduces its role in the arena of checks and balances. Life tenure for judges . . . and judicial review of enacted legislation are some of the . . . measures that may be necessary. In addition there has to be the executive which will implement and carry out court orders."[140]

Similarly, there is need to revise and strengthen political institutions, especially those designed to increase decentralization and regional autonomy within a federal system. *The Report of the Presidential Commission on Youth* found that there is throughout Sri Lanka "widespread consensus that devolution is a necessary and important aspect of any future political framework and that the process of devolution should not only include Provincial Councils but should go beyond it to ensure meaningful participation at the local level."[141]

The commission also advocates restructuring education as well as certain public practices in keeping with the imperatives of tolerance. "The representations made in Jaffna were unanimous in their belief that the alienation of the Tamil community began in 1956 with the Sinhala Only Act. Tamil nationalism in Sri Lanka, as in India, has its roots in perceived linguistic discrimination."[142]

Accordingly, the commission recommends extending the teaching and practice of bilingualism throughout the society. For example, from grades 3 to 6, Sinhala children should learn Tamil and Tamil children Sinhala in order to expose them to the language and culture of the other community. Beyond grade 6, the option to pursue the study of each other's language should be made available in all schools.[143] Textbooks and educational materials in the two languages should be inspected for all traces of cultural bias and favoritism and systematically revised to contribute to national harmony."[144] Specifically, students should be introduced both to their own cultural heritage and to the heritage of other groups in the society. Such introduction should include being exposed "to the places of worship, rituals and practices of other religions so as to increase awareness and tolerance."[145] Teachers and students should be exchanged regularly between the north and the south.[146]

Public media should be more ethnically sensitive. Television and radio programs should "cater to a multiethnic audience." Subtitles in the opposite language should be displayed on films and television as a standard practice. There ought to be joint radio programs in Sinhala and Tamil, and the print media also should help "to create an awareness of the customs and practices of all communities."[147]

Finally, the ethnically divisive ideologies that have gripped and motivated so many Sinhala and Tamils, particularly so many of the youth, must be critically reexamined and rethought. "The ideologies that proliferate today and which have captured the hearts and minds of our youth are 'the ideologies of the vernacular.'" They have grown out of "the symbols, discourse and mythology of Sinhala speaking and Tamil speaking intellectuals,"[148] and they have, in their extreme form, given support and inspiration to the radical nationalism of militant groups such as the JVP and the LTTE. These ideologies are in their various ways "animated by a unitary totalitarian vision," which has little room for liberal, pluralistic values and mutual respect for the equal worth of all people. Too much attention has been lavished on "dynastic history," on tales of "magnificent kings who fought with valour and swords."[149] Heroes of another kind should be singled out and celebrated—heroes, whether ancient or modern, who have supported tolerance, mutual understanding, and inclusiveness. Dwelling on heroes of that sort can perhaps help to make "the democratic alternative an attractive one for the South Asian imagination."[150]

*seven*

# Conclusion

It is sometimes said that the conflict in Sri Lanka is not religious,[1] but ethnic and linguistic, and that considerations of religious tolerance and intolerance are therefore not as pertinent as other matters. This conclusion is partly right. The Sinhala majority has been at odds with, and has from time to time discriminated against, the Tamil minority, but not because most Tamils are Hindus. Traditionally, Buddhists and Hindus have gotten on rather amicably in Sri Lanka. Buddhist temples coexist side by side with Hindu temples, and members of one community conventionally pay their respects to the other. Moreover, ethnicity often proves stronger than religion, as manifested, for example, in the abiding sense of distance between Sinhala and Tamil Christians.

While there is significant historical evidence of religious intolerance in Sri Lanka, such intolerance either has occurred between competing monastic groups within the Buddhist community or has resulted from the introduction of militant forms of Christianity associated with European colonialism, which began in the sixteenth century. Buddhists and Christians in Sri Lanka have occasionally displayed hostility toward one another, prompted in the first instance, no doubt, by the aggressive tactics of Christian missionaries.

The important point, however, is that the incidence of intolerance toward others because of their religious beliefs

and practices is not particularly germane to the central conflict that continues to divide and afflict Sri Lankan society.
Even when Buddhist monks or temples, or Hindu priests or
shrines, have been the object of violence in the civil war
between the Sinhala and the Tamils, it is more likely that
religious persons and places of worship were taken as offensive symbols or emblems of the despised opponent than that
they were attacked because of the religious beliefs and practices they represent.

On the other hand, if it is partly true that the conflict in
Sri Lanka is not about religion, that conclusion is at the same
time also partly—and crucially—mistaken. Religious belief
may not be a *target* of intolerance in reference to the conflict
between the Sinhala and the Tamils. Nevertheless, there can
be little doubt that religious belief has, for several reasons,
functioned in an important way as a *warrant* for intolerance
so far as the Sinhala Buddhists are concerned. There is also
evidence, though it is more controversial and perhaps less
pronounced, that the same is true for the Tamils.

Above all, the Sri Lankan case makes abundantly clear
why the distinction between two types of intolerance and
belief (target and warrant)[2]—a distinction of fundamental
importance to the general investigation of which this study
is a part—is indispensable for precise and accurate analysis.
True enough, Tamils and Sinhala may not have been targeted
for intolerant treatment because of their religious beliefs.
Nevertheless, specific religious texts, symbols, and legends,
whether Buddhist or Hindu (or Christian, for that matter)
have served, under certain conditions, as the justification and
inspiration for intolerance and discrimination.

Nor is it necessary, in cases in which religion functions
as a warrant for intolerance, that groups singled out for
intolerant treatment are selected on the basis of religion.
Ethnicity, language, cultural habits, and race may all serve,
singly or in combination, as a relevant badge of identity.
The key consideration is this: One group, however defined,
believes that it has religious authorization for declaring the
superiority and preeminence of its own language and cultural

tradition above others in a multiethnic society. When that group achieves power, it has, to its way of thinking, a legitimate reason for disregarding or minimizing the norms of nondiscrimination and equal treatment in implementing policies affecting education, employment, and other aspects of public life.

The Sinhala Buddhist revival movement, with its evolving attitude toward the Tamils, is a good example. In reaction to colonialism and emerging nationalism, the factors of race, language, and historical origins gained prominence as marks for distinguishing the Sinhala people from Tamils and others. But it was the religious factor—the sacred legends synthesized by Buddhist monks into the *Mahavamsa* and the other chronicles—that gave special authority to the Sinhala as a "chosen people" and thereby entitled them, from their point of view, to preserve and protect the special status, the proper preeminence, of the Sinhala Buddhist tradition in Sri Lankan life.[3]

Tamils were not disqualified only because most of them are Hindu. Along with other non-Sinhala Buddhist minorities, Tamil religion, language and culture was, at crucial historical junctures, disqualified from sharing "the foremost place" in Sri Lankan society simply because it is different from the Sinhala Buddhist tradition. As a particular racial, linguistic, and cultural community, the Sinhala, as they see it, have been invested with sacred political authority by the Buddhist tradition. It is precisely because of the centrality of race and language in that tradition that Sinhala Buddhist revivalism has never been particularly assimilationist toward Tamils and other groups. Non-Sinhala residents are acceptable and will be left alone so long as Sinhala Buddhist suzerainty is acknowledged.

There are, perhaps, some important parallels with Tamil revivalism, though that subject is less well investigated and documented. Probably in response to South Indian nationalism as well as to Sinhala revivalism and the policies of the Sri Lankan government derived therefrom, Tamil nationalists came to emphasize something of the same combination of race, language, and religious authorization that is so evident in the Sinhala tradition. The whole idea of a "Tamil homeland," embedded in a sacred past and warranted by religious and cultural loyalties, is reminiscent of Sinhala claims to the entitlements of antiquity. There are even occasional suggestions that the Tamils antedated the Sinhala as residents of primordial Sri Lanka, and therefore possess a prior warrant to rule the island as a whole.

At the same time, there are more limited claims in favor of exclusive Tamil control of a section of the country, namely, the northern and eastern provinces. The more limited claims are not, it is true, precisely parallel with Sinhala views. There is no analogue among the Sinhala Buddhists to Tamil separatism, according to which ethnic populations are segregated territorially.

Still, there is general symmetry between the two versions of revivalism in that each side considers the claims of the other to be, finally, a threat to its own basic legitimacy. Tamil separatism challenges the sacred integrity of the island unified under Buddhist suzerainty by Duttagamani in the second century B.C. Conversely, insistence upon Sinhala cultural and linguistic prerogatives challenges the treasured opportunities and distinctive identity of the Tamil community.

In calling attention to the role of religion in the ethnic strife that has afflicted Sri Lanka, it is by no means suggested that religion operates in a vacuum. The need of the Sinhala to revive and reassert what they believe are their sacred rights to shape Sri Lankan society is no doubt largely the result of the threat they have felt from the combined strength of Sri Lankan and South Indian Tamils, as well as from the disproportionate share of wealth and status that Tamils have at certain times been able to achieve. That and the special impact of colonial religious and political policies, as well as of the impulses of modern nationalism. Similarly, Sri Lankan Tamils have likely been prompted to draw upon the cultural and religious resources of South Indian nationalism in response to perceived economic and political deprivations experienced at the hands of the Sinhala majority.

On the other hand, the fact that religion is influenced by political and economic interests ought not obscure the importance of one of the characteristic roles of religion, which is to provide justification for social and political arrangements. Whatever else it is, the conflict in Sri Lanka is over competing and mutually exclusive beliefs about legitimate rule, which in turn are rooted in conflicting theories of sacred authority. In this sense, religion is *not* incidental to the continuing trouble in that country.

On the Sinhala side, at least, this fact accounts for the recurring political presence and influence of Buddhist monks. While it is important not to overrate the role of the monks in politics or to give the impression that the militants and the activists are more representative of the outlook of most monks than they are, it would be impossible to provide a complete description of Sri Lankan political history, certainly since the formative years of the late 1950s and the administration of S. W. R. D. Bandaranaike, without highlighting the impact of the bhikkhus.

That a certain number of monks is, under the right conditions, readily mobilizable in a public cause illustrates the profoundly political character of Sinhala Buddhism. The same thing is also illustrated by the successful electoral use Sinhala politicians such as the Bandaranaikes and J. R. Jayewardene have made of Buddhist themes in public life.

Of course, the fact that activist monks are typically a minority and that most monks avoid political involvement and consider it inappropriate points to the countervailing sense of reticence and suspicion toward politics that is a familiar characteristic of Buddhism. As president, Jayewardene in fact placed special emphasis on the tradition of nonattachment as a way of discouraging political interference by the monks.

Still, on balance it is the political significance of Buddhism— the triumph of revivalism, as it might be described—that has dominated the Sri Lankan story since the late nineteenth century. Revivalism emerged as a reaction to several factors—to British colonialism and to the rise of modern nationalism—

but it was also a response to and an adaptation of the ancient legacy of political Buddhism, influential in Sri Lanka, as well as in other parts of South Asia.

> Traditionally, the overarching cosmological and ideological frameworks of the (Buddhist) peoples of Sri Lanka, Burma, Thailand, and so on were predicated on a shared formula: that there is a special relationship between the *sangha* . . . and the polity, between the Buddhist quest for salvation of the renouncer and the Buddhist lay ethic of the wider society of householders capped by kingship. . . . [The king's role] was to institutionally support, materially nurture, and physically protect the *sangha* as the exemplar that guarantees the dignity and authenticity of the whole. In this larger formulation, the ideology linked the religion *(sasana)* with the polity, and acclaimed it as the special heritage and destiny of the people—the Sinhalese, the Burmese, the Mons, the Thais, the Laos, and so on—who were shaped to think of themselves as a "race" cum "nation," with a special historical mission indissolubly linked with Buddhism. This framework, this mold, was constructed and set in place at the critical phases when, at various times, these Buddhist polities attained their political consolidation, and claimed their religious and moral legitimacy from Buddhist monastic communities which . . . acted as civilizing agents in the expanding periphery. The monks in turn required the patronage of rulers to secure their material needs, and to guarantee their safety from invaders and the vagaries of political uncertainty and instability.[4]

Under the segmented and only very loosely connected social and political relations of premodern society, religious, linguistic, and cultural diversity flourished, so that the favored relation between ruler and sangha caused minimal friction. However, as societies like Sri Lanka consolidated and standardized themselves under the modern imperatives of colonialism and nationalism, the dominant political Buddhist model, partly influenced and propelled in the Sri Lankan case by revivalist resentments and racial doctrines, became more assertive and intrusive. In its modern version and in its new setting, the model more readily generated resistance and hard feelings among non-Buddhists. It is by this process that political Buddhism helped to contribute to the "invention of enmity" in Sri Lanka.

To the extent that Tamil nationalism, for its part, mirrors comparable beliefs and commitments in defense of a policy of separation and suspicion toward the Sinhala, it has helped to make a similar contribution.

Working to modify and revise those beliefs that have become warrants for intolerance and discrimination appears to be an urgent piece of business for all Sri Lankans. Making the right changes will help to bring attitudes and practices on every side into closer accommodation with the norms enshrined in the human rights instruments, including the UN Declaration against Intolerance, that systematically exclude race, color, language, religion, national or social origin, and other characteristics as bases for discrimination and preferential treatment in the public order.

Attempts in the past to modify beliefs in keeping with a more cosmopolitan outlook, as for example under British rule or during the administration of D. S. Senanayake, were halfhearted and ineffective. The British, whose policies were never entirely free of their own brand of cultural, racial, and religious superiority, were not exemplary tutors. Nor were they particularly sensitive to the menace of ethnocentrism, which in various ways they inadvertently encouraged rather than restrained.

As a matter of fact, Senanayake, in the years immediately after independence, manifested something of the same casual British attitude toward the profound challenge and difficulty of moving Sri Lanka in a more cosmopolitan direction. This despite his own strong personal disdain for communal rivalries. Like the British, he trusted in the capacity of the anglicized elite to take charge, and, like the British, he misjudged the character and dynamics of the revivalist phenomenon that was gathering power under his nose.

What seems called for now is precisely what was lacking earlier: the sort of concerted, resolute, and wide-ranging program of educational, social, political, legal, and cultural change elaborated in the 1990 *Report of the Presidential Commission on Youth*. In building on and elaborating the terms of peace sketched out in the Bandaranaike-Chelvanayagam pact and later entrenched in the Indo–Sri Lankan Agreement and the thirteenth and sixteenth amendments, the report captures the urgency and magnitude of the task.

There is, of course, a legitimate question as to how feasible such a recommendation is, especially when it is considered against the background of almost half a century of serious, and occasionally violent, ethnic tension. Clearly, important compromises will have to be made on both sides if a tolerant, pluralist society is to be achieved.

It is hard to see how continuing emphasis upon the ethnocentric policies of Sinhala Buddhist revivalism, so much a part of recent Sri Lankan history, can help assuage ethnic enmity, particularly if the Sinhala majority attempts to implement those policies by means of its considerable electoral advantage. By the same token, it is hard to see, in regard to the Tamil point of view, how separatism or, for that matter, how any claims to exclusive Tamil control over an ethnically segregated region, would in the long run enhance the prospects for multiethnic cooperation. A policy of ethnic exclusivity would not appear to advance the cause of mutuality any better than a policy of ethnic superiority.

As a matter of fact, however, there is in the record some basis for hope. It is well to recall that the Bandaranaike-Chelvanayagam pact of 1957—the basis for what many reasonable people see as a solution to the Sri Lankan civil war—was struck during a period of intense ethnocentrism, especially on the part of the Sinhala, and that the very Bandaranaike who agreed to the terms of the pact was the same person who had so shamelessly capitalized on extremism a short time before in the election of 1956.

This suggests that ethnic tension in Sri Lanka is a highly ambivalent matter. The stimulants of conflict are interconnected in a complex way with countervailing tendencies toward accommodation. The peaceful tendencies derive from a variety of sources. There is the precolonial, premodern pattern in Sri Lanka of cultural and religious intermingling and harmony based on a system of segmented social relations. Some observers contend that contemporary ethnic relations continue to be affected by this tradition to an important extent, as for example when Sinhala and Tamils go out of their way to protect and care for one another in the midst of ethnic violence.

There is the lingering and perhaps fitful influence of the "Asokan model" of religious tolerance, which is linked to an emphasis in the classical Buddhist texts on respect for other religions and points of view. This more benevolent and accommodating attitude toward outsiders appears to be gaining support among some of the younger university-educated monks, and that development may begin to counteract the ethnocentrism characteristic of militant monks of the 1950s and the 1980s.

There are also the transethnic cosmopolitan norms of equal treatment, freedom of conscience, and constitutional democracy, introduced by the British and so influential on the indigenous elites at the time of independence, individuals such as Senanayake and even Bandaranaike, to a lesser extent. That the British and postcolonial leaders like Senanayake did not go very far in disseminating and implementing the norms, or in effectively isolating the political system from ethnic consciousness, does not mean the norms can have no continuing or potential influence on ethnic developments in Sri Lanka. Reform of Sri Lankan political and legal institutions in keeping with broader provision for decentralization of authority, minority rights, nondiscrimination, and the like is a subject of ongoing, vigorous, and highly creative public discussion.

In addition, and perhaps most important, there is at present growing receptivity within the Sinhala and Tamil communities to many of the terms of ethnic cooperation, such as lingual equality, increased minority autonomy within a federal system, and respect for ethnic diversity. Receptivity to this degree would have been unimaginable earlier, despite the advertisement of those terms in documents like the Bandaranaike-Chelvanayagam pact. The increasing incidence of such tolerant attitudes is probably in part the result of widespread war-weariness, of general exhaustion from the tremendous psychic and material burdens of sustaining a civil war for such a long time. But it is also possibly influenced by a reawakening of some of the accommodationist themes that are an abiding if perhaps underutilized part of Sri Lankan experience.

In any case, while there is no immediate cause for great optimism that ethnic enmity can soon be set aside, there is also no cause for despair.

# Notes

## About the Series

**1.** Angelo Vidal d'Almeida Ribeiro, *Implementation of the Declaration on the Elimination of All Forms of Intolerance and of Discrimination Based on Religion or Belief*, report to the UN Commission on Human Rights, E/CN.4/1990/46, p. 58. "This background leads us to a brief reflection on the grim reality that the problem of intolerance and discrimination based on religion or belief is one of great magnitude today despite the existence of far-reaching guarantees of the right to freedom of thought, conscience, religion and belief in the constitutions of many states, of provisions to prevent and punish interference with legitimate manifestations of religious or beliefs in the laws and regulations of those States, and of continuing efforts on the part of Governments, religions, and beliefs, to foster tolerance by means of education. The problem involves not only discrimination negating rights and freedoms of individuals and groups of different religions and beliefs, but also attitudes and manifestations of intolerance between religions and beliefs, between individuals and groups having different religions and beliefs, as well as between nations and within nations" (Elizabeth Odio Benito, *Study of the Current Dimensions of the Problems of Intolerance and of Discrimination on Grounds of Religion or Belief*, UN Doc. E/CN.4/Sub.2/1987/26, p. 26).

**2.** D'Almeida Ribeiro, *Implementation of the Declaration*, p. 59.

**3.** Benito, *Study of Current Dimensions*, p. 39.

**4.** "As a result of lengthy discussions in various international bodies, it is now generally accepted that 'religion or belief' includes theistic, non-theistic, and atheistic belief" (ibid., p. 3).

**5.** See Donna Sullivan, "Advancing the Freedom of Religion or Belief through the UN Declaration on the Elimination of Religious Intolerance and Discrimination," *American Journal of International Law* 82 (1988): 504–506.

**6.** Sullivan, "Advancing Freedom of Religion," p. 505. "It has been realized that intolerance based on religion or belief has two separate aspects: first, an unfavorable attitude of mind towards persons or groups of a different religion or belief, and secondly, manifestations of such an attitude in practice. Such manifestations often take the form of discrimination, but in many cases they go much further and involve the stirring up of hatred against, or even the persecution of, individuals or groups of a different religion or belief" (Benito, *Study of Current Dimensions*, p. 3).

**7.** See for example, Nat Hentoff, "Stanford and the Speech Police," *Washington Post*, July 7, 1990, in which a policy against "discriminatory harassment" at Stanford University is criticized. This policy raises precisely the issue of perplexities concerning the proper limits of free speech. "A Stanford student is forbidden to use 'speech or other expression' that is 'intended to [directly] insult or stigmatize an individual or a small number of individuals on the basis of their sex, race, color, handicap, religion, sexual orientation or national and ethnic origin." Excluded are "fighting words"— words whose "very utterance inflict injury or tend to incite to an immediate breach of peace"—uttered against minorities. The regulation is interpreted not to protect the white majority from slanderous speech or gestures. Hentoff argues that such a regulation is hopelessly slippery. "Will a Stanford student suffer greater punishment for insulting an Italian-American in contrast to saying awful things to a Presbyterian?" He asserts that, by adopting such a policy, Stanford "has turned foolish and has forgotten why it and other colleges exist. Suppression of speech is not the reason, or it didn't use to be."

**8.** So long as we remember what we are doing, the convenience of using one word—intolerance—to cover both attitudes and practices as a kind of shorthand is considerable and fully in line with ordinary usage. In common speech, patterns of religious discrimination and persecution provide evidence for the existence of intolerance. That is true, no doubt, because, as the preceding discussion points out, to discriminate against or to persecute an individual or a group appears to be one important way of giving expression to intolerance. For analytical purposes, it is still open, of course, to specify the more refined meaning of intolerance (in regard specifically to attitudes) where such distinctions are important.

9. James Madison substituted "the concept of freedom of conscience for the . . . idea of toleration. The difference was dramatically stated by Thomas Paine: 'Toleration is not the opposite of intolerance, but it is the counterfeit of it. Both are despotisms. The one assumes to itself the right of withholding liberty of conscience, the other of granting it. The one is the pope armed with fire and faggot, the other is the pope selling or granting indulgences'" (Robert L. Ketchum, "James Madison and Religion: A New Hypothesis," *James Madison on Religious Liberty*, edited by Robert S. Alley [Buffalo, N.Y.: Prometheus Books, 1985], pp. 187–188).

10. See D. W. Hamlyn, *The Theory of Knowledge* (Garden City, N.Y.: Doubleday & Co., 1970), pp. 86–95.

11. Niccolo Machiavelli, *The Prince and the Discourses* (New York: Modern Library, 1950), pp. 65–66.

12. Max Weber, "The Meaning of Discipline," in *From Max Weber: Essays in Sociology*, edited by H. H. Gerth and C. Wright Mills (New York: Oxford University Press, 1958), p. 262.

13. Sullivan, "Advancing Freedom of Religion," pp. 492ff.

14. If a convincing case can be made that the public expression of a belief constitutes a direct incitement to rebellion, then that is usually considered a justified reason for punishing or suppressing the public expression of that belief. The difficulties arise when a government is suspected of using its accepted authority to suppress sedition as a pretext for suppressing unseditious criticism.

## 1. Introduction

1. John D. Rogers, "Regionalism and Ethnicity in Sri Lanka," expanded version of the paper presented to the working group conference, p. 1.

2. Donald L. Horowitz, "Making Moderation Pay: The Comparative Politics of Ethnic Conflict Management," in *Conflict and*

*Peacemaking in Multiethnic Societies,* edited by Joseph V. Montville (Lexington, Mass.: Lexington Books, 1990), pp. 459–460.

3. Rogers, "Regionalism and Ethnicity in Sri Lanka," original paper presented to the working group conference, p. 13.

4. Radhika Coomaraswamy, *Sri Lanka: The Crisis of the Anglo-American Constitutional Traditions in a Developing Society* (New Delhi: Vikas Publishing House, 1984), pp. 23, 24.

5. K. M. de Silva, *Managing Ethnic Tensions in Multi-Ethnic Societies: Sri Lanka, 1880–1983* (Washington, D.C.: University Press of America, 1986), p. 288.

6. Rogers, "Regionalism and Ethnicity," p. 16.

7. Steven Kemper, "J. R. Jayewardene, Righteousness and *Realpolitik*," in *Sri Lanka: History and the Roots of Conflict,* edited by Jonathan Spencer (London: Routledge, 1991), p. 200.

8. K. M. de Silva, *India in Sri Lanka, 1983–1991* (Occasional Paper, Woodrow Wilson Center, February 5, 1992), p. 8.

9. Sarath Amunugama, "Buddhaputra and Bhumiputra? Dilemmas of Modern Sinhala Buddhist Monks in Relation to Ethnic and Political Conflict," unpublished version of the paper presented to the working group conference, p. 1. For a published version, see *Religion* 21 (1991): 115–139.

## 2. Background of Sinhala Identity

1. A subtle scholarly debate has developed, of late, between R. A. L. H. Gunawardena ("The People of the Lion: The Sinhala Identity and Ideology in History and Historiography," in *Sri Lanka: History and the Roots of Conflict*) and K. M. O. Dharmadasa ("The People of the Lion: Ethnic Identity, Ideology, and Historical Revisionism in Contemporary Sri Lanka," unpublished essay). The debate is over how ancient the precedents for Sinhala and Tamil ethnic identity were. Gunawardena inclines to locate them in the tenth century A.D., while Dharmadasa finds precedents as early as the fifth century A.D. In an illuminating discussion of the differences, Stanley Tambiah decides that "there seems to be ultimately greater convergence between Gunawardena and Dharmadasa than might appear at first sight when their radical claims are qualified by their sense of identity formation (Sinhala, and Sinhala Buddhist) as an expanding temporal process." Stanley Jeyaraja

Tambiah, *Buddhism Betrayed? Religion, Politics, and Violence in Sri Lanka* (Chicago: University of Chicago Press, 1992), p. 137.

2. Rogers, "Regionalism and Ethnicity" expanded comments, p. 6: "I believe that these overarching ethnic identities, at least in their present forms, are modern (or [British] colonial) creations." Rogers, transcript of the working group conference [hereafter, transcript], p. 5: "The direct British role in constructing identities came in the early middle nineteenth century." "It was during the period of colonial rule that the Sinhala consciousness underwent a radical transformation and began to assume its current form," Gunawardena, "People of the Lion," p. 33. See George Bond's comments, transcript, p. 5. Cf. Elizabeth Nissan and R. L. Stirrat, "The Generation of Communal Identities," in *Sri Lanka: History and the Roots of Conflict*, p. 31.

3. See "About the Series," pp. xxvi–xxvii, for a discussion of a central distinction between two ways that belief and intolerance go together: belief as the target of intolerance, and belief as a warrant for intolerance.

As will become apparent, it is the second kind of intolerance—belief as warrant for intolerance—that is particularly salient in the ethnic conflict that develops in the nineteenth and twentieth centuries in Sri Lanka. Still, the practice of targeting groups for mistreatment because of their religion, a practice introduced by the Portuguese and Dutch and expanded by the British, is an important part of the history of intolerance in Sri Lanka. As we shall see, intolerance of the first sort, namely using public benefits and burdens as an explicit means of favoring one religious group and disadvantaging others, created a climate of resentment and hostility that eventually helped to encourage intolerance of the second sort.

4. For example, they made much use of baptism as a condition for receiving civil and economic privileges. See Kitsiri Malalgoda, *Buddhism in Sinhalese Society* (Berkeley: University of California Press, 1976), p. 207.

5. "Under the Dutch regime the principle of official support of the established religion carried with it the obligation to discourage, if not suppress, the public practice of other religions; and in particular it included the promulgation and implementation of rigorous laws against the Roman Catholics. Membership in the Dutch Reformed Church had been made a prerequisite for securing state employment and for preferment therein" (K. M. de Silva, *Religion,*

*Nationalism and the State in Modern Sri Lanka,* USF Monographs in Religion and Public Policy, no. 1 [Tampa, Fla.: University of South Florida, 1986], p. 7).

**6.** K. M. de Silva, *Managing Ethnic Tensions,* pp. 17–18.

**7.** Kemper, *The Presence of the Past: Chronicles, Politics, and Culture in Sinhala Life* (Ithaca, N.Y.: Cornell University Press, 1991), pp. 40–41: "Doctrinal dispute was nothing new when [King] Mahasena came to power some three centuries after Christ. What was new was his active suppression of the Mahavihara [a Theravadin monastic community], although the Mahayana or proto-Mahayana monks had themselves [previously] been suppressed by Gothabhaya (249–62 B.C.)." As Kemper points out, suppression involved the exile of monks who were out of favor, forced evacuation and demolition of monasteries, and even the occasional execution of a monastic leader.

"Buddhism, like all great religious traditions, has dealt with difficulty with the problems of schism, sectarianism, and heresy. While tolerant of other faiths, popular and sophisticated, and while able to incorporate and transform indigenous elements, Sinhalese Buddhism has persistently felt threatened by the specter of heretical movements from within. In the words of G. P. Malalasekere: 'To the assaults of open opponents the Buddhist displays the calmest indifference, convinced that in its undiminished strength his faith is firm and inexpungable; his vigilance is only excited by the alarm of internal dissent, and all his passions are aroused to stifle the symptoms of schism.'" (Bardwell L. Smith, "The Ideal Social Order as Portrayed in the Chronicles of Ceylon," in *Religion and the Legitimation of Power,* edited by Smith [Chambersburg, Pa.: Anima Books, 1978], p. 52).

**8.** Private conversation with K. M. de Silva, Washington, D.C., July 16, 1992. In an as-yet unpublished review of two essays on "Buddhist Fundamentalism" by Donald Swearer and James Manor, Professor de Silva elaborates as follows: "The entry of the Portuguese on the Sri Lankan scene in the 16th century saw the entry also of Roman Catholicism and religious intolerance of the Counter-Reformation into an island whose Buddhist society was well-known for its religious tolerance." And in his essay "Buddhist Revivalism, Nationalism, and Politics in Modern Sri Lanka" (in *Fundamentalism, Revivalists and Violence in South Asia,* edited by James Warner Bjorkman [Riverdale, Md.: Riverdale Company, 1988], p. 109), de Silva adds: "Portuguese colonialism was very much the child of the counter-reformation. If its emphasis on the principle of [*cujus regio, ejus religio*] perpetuated a central feature of the Sri Lankan political system—since the local link between state and religion had originated as long ago as the third century BC—the zealotry and harsh intolerance which characterized the imposition of Roman Catholicism on Sri Lanka were something new and unfamiliar. *Sri Lankan society and civilization had seldom confused the obligation to encourage adherence to the national religion with the suppression of other faiths*" (emphasis added).

9. Nissan and Stirrat, "Generation of Communal Identities," p. 26.

10. Stanley Tambiah, transcript, p. 10. "The spirit of intolerance came to Sri Lanka with the Portuguese" (K. M. de Silva, review of essays by Swearer and Manor).

11. Michael Ames, "Westernization or Modernization: The Case of Sinhalese Buddhism," *Social Compass* 20, 2 (1973) 141, cited in George D. Bond, *The Buddhist Revival in Sri Lanka. Religious Tradition, Reinterpretation, and Response* (Columbia: University of South Carolina Press, 1988), p. 21.

12. "British rule . . . began with a general and deliberate relaxation of [the preceding] policies, if not a repudiation of many of them. The compelling motive behind this reversal of policies was not the simple one of a commitment to the abstract principle of religious toleration. There were practical advantages expected from this, in particular the hope that this would enable the British to win the adherence of groups discontented with the harsh policies of the Dutch" (K. M. de Silva, *Religion, Nationalism and the State*, p. 7). The one exception was the first governor, Frederick North (1798–1805), who "took the initiative in [reorganizing missionary efforts], and [manifested] . . . enthusiasm for the propagation of Christianity" (Malalgoda, *Buddhism in Sinhalese Society*, p. 191). However, thanks to mistaken Dutch statistics on religious affiliation, North was under the misapprehension that he was dealing with a largely Christian population (K. M. de Silva, *Religion, Nationalism and the State*, p. 8). North's immediate successors modified his policies when they saw that the population was by no means generally Christian.

13. See Malalgoda, "Buddhism versus Christianity: Beginnings of Buddhist Protest," chap. 6 in *Buddhism in Sinhalese Society*.

14. Richard Gombrich, "Protestant Buddhism," in *Theravada Buddhism: A Social History from Ancient Benares to Modern Colombo*

(London: Routledge & Kegan Paul, 1988), cited on p. 178 from a description in 1823 of the work of a Methodist missionary.

**15.** Ibid., p. 179.

**16.** "It is worth noting that the lack of governmental assistance did not lead to the extinction of the Buddhist monastic schools; in fact, the general decline which was manifest in the Kandyan provinces had no impact on the low country, where there was a steady strengthening of monastic education in the course of the nineteenth century. But, even at their best, Buddhist monastic schools were no match for Christian schools so far as the educational needs of laymen were concerned. Christian schools alone, with their more modern curricula, English education, and formal and informal contacts with the administration, had the capacity to provide laymen with secure avenues of secular advancement" (ibid., p. 196).

**17.** Bond, *Buddhist Revival*, pp. 16–17.

**18.** By the 1830s, a strong evangelical impulse began to affect the Colonial Office in England, leading it to give "its support to the propagation of Christianity in Sri Lanka" and to encourage "the government there to adopt this as part of its official obligations" (K. M. de Silva, *Religion, Nationalism and the State*, p. 8).

**19.** Malalgoda, *Buddhism in Sinhalese Society*, pp. 193–196.

**20.** K. M. de Silva, "Buddhist Revivalism, Nationalism, and Politics," p. 111.

**21.** K. M. de Silva, review of essays by Swearer and Manor, p. 5. The eventual disestablishment of Anglicanism in 1881, and the withdrawal of ecclesiastical subsidies, was a result of a long-standing campaign waged especially by the Methodists and Baptists for implementing a policy of religious liberty and equal treatment of Christian groups in the mission field (K. M. de Silva, *Religion, Nationalism and the State*, pp. 13–14).

**22.** The book was written by a Methodist missionary, R. Spence Hardy, as cited in Gombrich, "Protestant Buddhism," p. 176.

**23.** Ibid.

**24.** K. M. de Silva, *Religion, Nationalism and the State*, p. 11.

**25.** K. M. de Silva, "Buddhist Revivalism," p. 112.

**26.** Even though the colonial government adopted a more cooperative attitude toward the Buddhists in the 1880s, "Buddhist monks were not quite ready . . . to make use of the new sympathetic attitude of the government," especially with respect to education (Malalgoda, *Buddhism in Sinhalese Society*, pp. 235–237).

**27.** Tambiah called attention to the importance of the language of racism in the development of the idea of Sinhala identity (transcript, p. 10).

**28.** William Knighton, who published *History of Ceylon from the Earliest Period to the Present Time in 1845.*

**29.** Rogers, "Historical Images in the British Period," in *Sri Lanka: History and the Roots of Conflict,* pp. 90–92.

**30.** Gunawardena, "The People of the Lion: The Sinhala Identity and Ideology in History and Historiography," in *Sri Lanka: History and the Roots of Conflict,* p. 73.

**31.** Bond, *Buddhist Revival,* p. 21.

**32.** James Alwis, cited in ibid., p. 22.

**33.** Malalgoda, *Buddhism in Sinhalese Society,* pp. 213–215. Government compliance with the suggestion was "a very rare occurrence" (p. 215). On one occasion, a governor urged the Wesleyan mission to withdraw a tract because of the "hostile feelings" it conveyed. It was acceptable, he said, that "true Religion" be maintained against "spurious religion," but in a less offensive manner. According to Malalgoda, the government did worry about antagonizing the Buddhists, and the British were somewhat embarrassed about neglecting their obligations under the Kandyan Convention. "Their basic attitudes towards Buddhism, however, did not differ significantly from those of the missionaries; all of them, to varying degrees were supporters of the missionary enterprise; most of them had the same vision as the missionaries of a Buddhism that was doomed to decline and fall" (p. 215).

**34.** Gombrich, "Protestant Buddhism," p. 180.

**35.** Ibid.

**36.** Ibid., p. 181.

**37.** Cited in Malalgoda, *Buddhism in Sinhalese Society,* pp. 224–225.

**38.** Gombrich, "Protestant Buddhism," p. 182; cf. Bond, *Buddhist Revival,* pp. 47–48.

**39.** Gombrich, "Protestant Buddhism," p. 182.

**40.** Bond, transcript, pp. 1–3. Cf. Bond, *Buddhist Revival,* chaps. 1, 2.

**41.** "The direct British role in constructing identities came in the early and middle nineteenth century. And the Buddhist

revival—which was in part a response to the whole colonial society—took those [colonial] categories as one of the starting points
and refashioned them in its own way" (Rogers, transcript, p. 5).
"In keeping with the general theme of fashioning identities, we
should note that this [Buddhist] revival, which occurred in the late
nineteenth and twentieth centuries, was primarily a search for
identity. This was not just a search for political identity, but an
identity that would enable the Sinhalese to redefine their existence
in terms of Buddhist principles. [As the result of] colonial rule,
the Buddhist identity was not a given" (Bond, transcript, p. 1).

42. Rogers, "Social Mobility," p. 588.

43. "In Sri Lanka as in many parts of Asia the origins of modern
nationalism can be traced back to programs of religious revivalism
which were a reaction against missionary enterprise. Religious
revival—a buddhist revival, more specifically—preceded the emergence of political nationalism on the island. It contributed greatly
to the latter by providing as it did an ideal basis for the rejection
of the pervasive occidental presence and influence in Sri Lankan
society" (K. M. de Silva, *Managing Ethnic Tensions*, p. 31).

# 3. Sinhala Buddhist Revivalism

1. Nissan and Stirrat, "Generation of Communal Identities," p. 41.

2. Gananath Obeysekere first employed this term in 1970
("Religious Symbolism and Political Change in Ceylon," *Modern
Ceylon Studies* 1: 43–63). It has also been employed by Malalgoda
(*Buddhism in Sinhalese Society*), by Bond (*Buddhist Revival*), and by
Gombrich ("Protestant Buddhism"). The accuracy of this term has
been challenged by John C. Holt, "Protestant Buddhism?" *Ethnic
Studies Report* 9, 1 (1990): 1–8, and "Protestant Buddhism?" *Religious
Studies Review* 17, 4 (October 1991): 307–312. K. M. de Silva has
also cast doubt on the term in his review of essays by Swearer
and Manor, as does H. L. Seneviratne in his review of Gombrich
and Obeysekere, *Buddhism Transformed: Religious Change in Sri Lanka*
(Princeton: Princeton University Press, 1988), in *Journal of Ritual
Studies* 4, 2 (Summer 1990): Whereas the Protestant Reformation
involved "detraditionalization, rationalization and demagicization
('disenchantment'), the overwhelming majority of the Protestant
Buddhists [in Sri Lanka] . . . remain rhapsodied in magic and traditionalism" (p. 401). To add to the controversy, George Bond in

correspondence questions the interpretation of the term "Protestant Buddhism" presented in the following pages. The term, he suggests, is to be understood not so much as implying that the Buddhists imitated and borrowed from the Protestant missionaries of nineteenth century Sri Lanka, but that they worked out "a reformist interpretation [of Buddhism] much like [that of] the Protestant reformers [of the sixteenth century]." Two things may be said in response: There is probable evidence of borrowing and influence from the missionaries (see Malalgoda, *Buddhism in Sinhalese Society*, p. 226, and Tambiah, *Buddhism Betrayed?* p. 7); the continuing allegiance of Sri Lankan Buddhism to monasticism as well as to "magic and traditionalism" despite its other reforms would detract from the pertinence of the term "Protestant," whether it is nineteenth-century missionaries or sixteenth-century reformers that are being considered.

3. Malalgoda, *Buddhism in Sinhalese Society*, pp. 246, 260; Bond, *Buddhist Revival*, pp. 36, 61ff.

4. The phrase is K. M. de Silva's, used to describe one of the leading revivalists, Anagarika Dharmapala (see below) (review of essays by Swearer and Manor).

5. Amunugama, "Anagarika Dharmapala (1864–1933) and the Transformation of Sinhala Buddhist Organization in a Colonial Setting," *Social Science Information* 24 (1985), p. 720. Cf. Bond, *Buddhist Revival*, pp. 34ff. "One basic theme of all the Sinhalese revivalists ... has been what Tambiah terms 'an accent on scripturalism.'" While this is unquestionably a new emphasis, one should not forget Bond's reminder that "Theravada has a history of scripturalist purifications of religion going as far back as Asoka's legendary purification of the Sangha."

6. Bond, *Buddhist Revival*, p. 34. Though, H. L. Seneviratne points out that it was only after the texts were translated into English or Sinhala that the monks could read them. Very few read Pali.

7. Tambiah, *Buddhism Betrayed?*, p. 7.

8. Holt, "Protestant Buddhism?" (1991), p. 309.

9. Ibid.

10. Ibid. If anything, says Holt, this tendency to display religious images in public would correspond more closely to Roman Catholicism than to Protestantism. Indeed, the neglect of the Catholic

influence on Buddhism is part of Holt's complaint about the use of the term "Protestant Buddhism."

**11.** "In a life of fifty years of agitation and exhortation he fashioned a philosophy which, while drawing from traditional heritage, was contemporary in that it enabled the Sinhalese to confront present realities. In sum, Dharmapala attempted to redefine the new identity of Sinhalese Buddhists within a pluralistic, colonial society" (Amunugama, "Anagarika Dharmapala," p. 713).

**12.** The primary source for this summary of the life and thought of Dharmapala is Amunugama, "Anagarika Dharmapala." pp. 697–730. Cf. Bond, *Buddhist Revival,* pp. 53–70; Gombrich, "Protestant Buddhism," 188–197.

**13.** From Dharmapala's *Return to Righteousness,* edited by A. Guruge (Colombo: Government Press, 1965), p. 684, cited in Amunugama, "Anagarika Dharmapala," p. 703.

**14.** Ibid.

**15.** Obeyesekere, "The Problem of Fundamentalism in a Non-Monotheistic Religion: The Case of Theravada Buddhism," unpublished paper, p. 9.

**16.** Cited in Malalgoda, *Buddhism in Sinhalese Society,* p. 244.

**17.** Ibid.

**18.** In the interests of encouraging Indian nationalism, Colonel Olcott favored the triumph of Hinduism in India and therefore gave greater support to Hinduism than Buddhism—a development that turned Dharmapala away from Theosophy. See Amunugama, "A Sinhala Buddhist 'Babu': Anagarika Dharmapala (1864–1933) and the Bengal Connection," *Social Science Information* 30 (198?), pp. 18–19.

**19.** Gunawardena, "People of the Lion," in *Sri Lanka: History and the Roots of Conflict,* p. 76.

**20.** For a fascinating account of Dharmapala's influence on certain early-twentieth-century Sinhalese novelists, such as Sirisena, and thereby on "the creation of a new Sinhala Buddhist constituency in Sri Lanka" among the Sinhala intelligentsia, see Amunugama, "Ideology and Class Interest in One of Piyadasa Sirisena's Novels: The New Image of the 'Sinhala Buddhist' Nationalist," Chapter 8 in *Collective Identities, Nationalisms and Protest in Modern Sri Lanka,* edited by Michael Roberts (Colombo, 1979), pp. 314–336.

21. K. M. de Silva, *Managing Ethnic Tensions*, pp. 41–42. Cf. K. M. de Silva, *Religion, Nationalism and the State*, p. 20.

22. Bond, *Buddhist Revival in Sri Lanka*, p. 60.

23. K. M. de Silva, "Buddhist Revivalism," p. 120.

24. Borrowed from the title of Sarath Amunugama's paper presented to the working group conference: "Buddhaputra and Bhumiputra [Sons of Buddha and Sons of the Soil]? Dilemmas of Modern Sinhala Buddhist Monks in Relation to Ethnic and Political Conflict."

25. Cited in Kumari Jayawardena, *Ethnic and Class Conflicts in Sri Lanka* (Colombo: Sanjiva Books, 1990), pp. 18–19.

26. Cited in Amunugama, "Anagarika Dharmapala," p. 715.

27. Ibid., p. 716.

28. Rogers, "Regionalism and Ethnicity," expanded comments, p. 22: "Sri Lanka must be the only country in the world where the front pages of the newspapers constantly carry 1,000 or 2,500 year old news (e.g., Sinhalese-Buddhist ruins found in Jaffna)."

29. Cited in Bond, *Buddhist Revival*, p. 55.

30. Cited in Kemper, *Presence of the Past*, p. 199.

31. Ibid., p. 125.

32. Cited in Bond, *Buddhist Revival*, p. 55.

33. Cited in Kemper, *Presence of the Past*, p. 200.

34. The *Dipavamsa* was probably compiled in the fourth century A.D., and is of unknown authorship. Compared with the *Mahavamsa*, which was probably composed in the sixth century A.D. by a monk named Mahanama, it is a relatively prosaic and primitive account. However, there are some interesting contrasts between the two chronicles, as we shall see. Sections of the *Culavamsa* were written in the twelfth, thirteenth, and eighteenth centuries, and is an extension of the *Mahavamsa*.

35. Walpola Rahula, *History of Buddhism in Ceylon*, pp. xxiii–xxiv, cited in Alice Greenwald, "The Relic on the Spear: Historiography and the Saga of Duttagamani," in *Religion and the Legitimation of Power*, p. 13. As Rahula puts it, "Both the *Dipavamsa* and the *Mahavamsa* are histories of Buddhism. In them secular history is subservient to religious history" (cited at p. 13).

36. Smith, "Ideal Social Order."

37. "Charter is conceived of in the Malinowskian sense as that which, through the medium of myth (or, in this case, religious historiography), both engenders and substantiates a cultural self-consciousness" (Greenwald, "Relic on the Spear," p. 14).

38. The notion of the "resonance" of themes and concerns in the chronicles with nineteenth- and twentieth-century "nationalist visions" is drawn from Kemper, *Presence of the Past*, p. 195.

39. Heinz Bechert, "The Beginnings of Buddhist Historiography: Mahavamsa and Political Thinking," in *Religion and the Legitimation of Power*, p. 7.

40. As Heinz Bechert remarks, the "authors of the chronicles were [Theravada] Buddhist monks. It is surprising at first sight that bhikkhus should have been the propagators of a state ideology, when we recall the rule of the Order. We know, however, that religious ideas always have occupied an important place in the traditional state ideology of a Theravada Buddhist kingdom. The king was customarily described as a *cakravartin*, i.e., as a universal monarch as described in canonical Buddhist works. He was also identified as a *bodhisattva*, i.e., a Buddha-to-be, and his Buddhist legitimation was bound to his function as a promoter and protector of orthodox Theravada Buddhism." Ibid., p. 8.

41. Kemper, *Presence of the Past*, p. 3. Kemper's observation is about the *Mahavamsa*, but it could be said of all the chronicles.

42. *The Mahavamsa, or The Great Chronicle of Ceylon*, trans. by Wilhelm Geiger (Colombo: Government Publications Bureau, 1960), 1: 43.

43. Ibid. 1: 20.

44. Ibid. 7: 3–4.

45. Regina T. Clifford, "The Dhammadipa Tradition of Sri Lanka: Three Models within the Sinhalese Chronicles," in *Religion and the Legitimation of Power*, p. 41.

46. In contrast to the *Dipavamsa*, which treats Duttagamani rather hastily, the *Mahavamsa* devotes all of 861 verses to him. "He is the hero Vijaya cannot quite be and the paradigm of the righteous Buddhist king. With his career Mahanama [the author of the *Mahavamsa*] finds a way [to interconnect] a political cause and a social identity" (Kemper, *Presence of the Past*, p. 60).

47. *Mahavamsa* 22: 63.

48. Ibid. 25: 17.

**49.** Ibid. 25: 109–11.

**50.** The interpretation of Buddhism associated with the chronicles "became a prominent view of the Buddhist revival." By that interpretation, the "protection of the Dharma [was bequeathed] to Vijaya, and the kings were depicted as the supporters and protectors of the Sangha.... Taking literally these chronicle myths, [the revivalists] could justify violence in defense of the Sangha" (Bond, transcript, p. 2).

**51.** From the *Pujavaliya*, "a Sinhalese prose work of the thirteenth century," quoted in Rahula, *History of Buddhism in Ceylon*, p. 63, cited in Greenwald, "Relic on the Spear," p. 24 (emphasis added).

**52.** Cited in Kemper, *Presence of the Past*, p. 200.

**53.** Ibid., pp. 199–200. "The nationalist reading of the Sri Lankan past depends on two figures, heroes and race, the first an ancient Sri Lankan notion justifiably traced back to the *Mahavamsa*, the second a Western idea imposed on Sri Lankan past by nineteenth-century scholars and nationalists. *The way these two figures interact seems to me to exemplify the influence of colonial culture on nationalist discourse, for the discursive formation that develops around heroes and races is neither simply Western nor local....* However seductive talk about Aryan languages and races must have been for the Sinhala elite of the nineteenth and twentieth centuries, the cult of heroes made that talk even more seductive. On the one hand, the heroic careers of Vijaya and [Duttagamani] established the Sinhala's 'race's' antiquity as well as its rightful place in the emerging nation. On the other hand, every member of the race shared the blood of those heroic ancestors, and thus each was equally Sinhala and equally responsible for the common good" (pp. 106–107, emphasis added).

**54.** The term "segmentary state" is borrowed from the work of Burton Stein by Stirrat and Nissan, "Generation of Communal Identities," p. 25. They quote Stein: "The parts of which the state is composed are seen as prior to the formal state; these segments are structurally as well as morally coherent units in themselves. Together, these parts or segments comprise a state in recognition of a sacred ruler whose overlordship is of a moral sort and is expressed in an essentially ritual idiom" (from Stein, *Peasant, State and Society in South India* [Delhi, 1983], p. 23). In the same vein, H. L. Seneviratne remarks: "The model of political organization of the traditional order was what Tambiah has called 'galactic.' Here the units are not centralized, but centre oriented. They enjoyed substantial autonomy. Centralization was more symbolic than real, with the king styling himself as universal emperor, receiving ritual homage from the units which in reality managed their own affairs. ... Hegemony did not bring about hegemonization, as in the modern state. The ideology of Buddhist nationalism could continue without oppressing minority cultures" ("The Buddhist Historiographic Tradition in Sri Lanka," unpublished paper, p. 15).

**55.** Benedict Anderson, *Imagined Communities* (London: Verso, 1983), p. 26.

**56.** "One thing ... is clear: a primordial golden age with a perfect fit between Sinhala people, Sinhala language, Buddhism, and the entire territorial space of the island could not have existed in [Duttagamani's] time, and probably did not exist at the time the *Mahavamsa* was composed. Another historical process is equally clear: The Buddhacization and Sinhalization of people has been a continuing process through the centuries right up to the present time, and the genius of the island's civilization may well be located there as much as in the classical past when certain central postulates about the mutuality between kingship and sangha and their responsibility for the cultivation of Buddhist values in an agrarian society were articulated and pursued" (Tambiah, *Buddhism Betrayed?* p. 137).

**57.** Stirrat and Nissan, "Generation of Communal Identities," pp. 23–24. "Pre-colonial and most of colonial Sri Lankan history does not conform to the model of two opposed nations imposed upon it by present-day Tamil and Sinhala rhetoricians" (p. 24).

**58.** Interestingly enough, caste differences have continued to have an important impact on the sangha. "Entry into the most prestigious nikaya (sect) of the *sangha*, the *Siyam nikaya*, is restricted to the *goyigama* caste" (K. M. de Silva, *Managing Ethnic Tensions*, pp. 21–22).

**59.** Kemper, *Presence of the Past*, p. 71. According to Gunawardena, the *Mahavamsa* "embodies the message that the ksatriya status of the ruling family marks them out from people of all other ritual categories" ("People of the Lion," in *Sri Lanka: History and the Roots of Conflict*, p. 56).

**60.** Greenwald, "Relic on the Spear," pp. 21–23.

**61.** Kemper, *Presence of the Past*, p. 72. According to Gunawardena, the elements of the Vijaya myth in the *Mahavamsa* "are of crucial importance for understanding the nature of group consciousness that was developing in the period after the formation of a unified kingdom under the control of Anuradhapura. They enable us to distinguish the Sinhala consciousness of this early period from linguistic nationalism and other types of group consciousness typical of more recent times.... The Sinhala group consciousness did not bring together all speakers of the language but deliberately left out a considerable section of the linguistic group including the craftsmen-agriculturalists and others who performed ritually 'low' service functions" ("People of the Lion," in *Sri Lanka: History and the Roots of Conflict*, p. 55).

**62.** Kemper, *Presence of the Past*, p. 72.

**63.** See E. J. Hobsbawm, *Nations and Nationalism since 1780* (Cambridge: Cambridge University Press, 1991), chap. 3, "The Government Perspective." Cf. Ernest Gellner, *Nations and Nationalism* (Ithaca, N.Y.: Cornell University Press, 1983), especially chap. 2, "Industrial Society."

**64.** Amunugama, "Anagarika Dharmapala," p. 713 (emphasis added).

**65.** Rodolfo Stavenhagen, "Ethnic Conflicts and Their Impact on International Society," *International Social Science Journal* (February 1991): 120.

**66.** Amunugama, "Anagarika Dharmapala," p. 716 (emphasis added).

**67.** See ibid., pp. 716–727. Cf. Bond, *Buddhist Revival*, pp. 61–70. Amunugama comments: "While the sociologists writing on the Buddhist revival have, up to now, tended to emphasize the activities of laymen, *I propose to examine the writings of the principal 'actors' themselves. Col. Olcott for example recognized the centrality of the Sangha for Buddhist polity*" ("Anagarika Dharmapala," p. 717 [emphasis added]). Dharmapala's abiding concern for preserving monasticism, albeit a reformed version, is one reason why describing him as an advocate of "Protestant Buddhism" seems inaccurate. Protestantism is characteristically antimonastic.

**68.** Amunugama, "Anagarika Dharmapala," p. 719.

**69.** As George Bond emphasizes in correspondence, it is not Dharmapala alone who was responsible for recasting the Sri Lankan bhikkhu into a political and socially active form. There were people such as Mohottivatte Gunananda, who antedated Dharmapala, and some others who were his contemporaries (see Tambiah, *Buddhism Betrayed?* p. 6).

70. Amunugama, "Anagarika Dharmapala," p. 720.

71. Ibid., pp. 721–722.

72. Ibid., p. 722.

73. Rogers, "Regionalism and Ethnicity," expanded remarks, p. 12. See "About the Series," p. xxvi–xxvii.

74. Cited in Jayawardena, *Ethnic and Class Conflicts*, p. 24.

75. Amunugama, "Sinhala Buddhist 'Babu,'" p. 40.

76. Cited in Jayawardena, *Ethnic and Class Conflicts*, pp. 24–25.

77. K. M. de Silva, *Managing Ethnic Tensions*, p. 61.

78. Ibid.

79. Cited in Jayawardena, *Ethnic and Class Conflicts*, pp. 26–27.

80. Cited in Obeysekere, "Problem of Fundamentalism," p. 26.

81. K. M. de Silva, *Religion, Nationalism and the State*, p. 35 (emphasis added).

## 4. The Tamil Response

1. H. L. Seneviratne, "South Indian Cultural Nationalism and Separatism in Sri Lanka," paper presented to the working group conference, p. 22.

2. Seneviratne's thesis generated dispute during the conference. By his own account, he was making a proposal for further investigation rather than trying to settle things definitively. S. R. Perinbanayagam, the respondent to Seneviratne's paper, raised objections, though he found some parts of the argument plausible. Patrick Peebles had some further reservations. Other participants, like Stanley Tambiah, C. R. de Silva, and Vernon Mendis, tentatively concurred with Seneviratne. As it turns out, there is some interesting scholarly support for aspects of Seneviratne's thesis from authors such as Jane Russell, Dagmar Hellmann-Rajanayagam, Steven Kemper, Radhika Coomaraswamy, and some other Sri Lankan scholars, though here and there they suggest some interesting variations, as well. We shall take up the points of support, and a few of the suggested variations, as we go and then at the appropriate point attend to Perinbanayagam's and Peebles's criticisms.

3. Seneviratne, "South Indian Cultural Nationalism," pp. 22, 2.

**4.** Seneviratne adds: "By relating separatism to Tamil revivalism, I am not denying the validity of Tamil grievances arising from the excesses of Sinhalese chauvinist policies" (ibid., p. 2).

**5.** Seneviratne does not call attention to this difference in the kind of influence exerted by the missionaries on the Tamil and the Sinhala movements. Nor, beyond that, does he mention evidence of the negative side of missionary influence, which may also have affected the Tamils and which would more directly parallel the Sinhala case.

**6.** Ibid., pp. 2ff.

**7.** Ibid., p. 3.

**8.** Saiva Siddhanta is the Tamil school of Saivism, and Saivism, in turn, is a form of Hinduism distinct from Brahmanism. Brahmanism draws on the Vedas, an ancient collection of hymns, prayers, ritualistic descriptions, and the like. Saivism draws on a different body of ancient sacred literature, the Agamas. Saiva Siddhanta, in particular, is traceable to the teachings of Meykanda Devar, a thirteenth-century Saivist. The following description of Saiva Siddhanta from a modern source displays the continuing power of religious nationalism: "As a system of religious thought, as an expression of faith and life, the Saiva Siddhanta is by far the best South India possesses. *It represents not only in the South but in the whole of India the highest watermark of Indian thought and Indian life. It is the religion of the Tamil people, by the side of which every other form is of foreign origin*" (cited from an essay published in a Hindu student journal at the University of Peradeniya in Sri Lanka, 1959–60, in A. Sathasivam, "The Hindu Religious Heritage in Sri Lanka: Revived and Remembered," in *Religiousness in Sri Lanka*, edited by John Ross Carter [Colombo: Marga Institute, 1979], p. 167, emphasis added). Cf. Coomaraswamy, "Myths without Conscience: Tamil and Sinhalese Nationalist Writings in the 1980s," in *Facets of Ethnicity in Sri Lanka*, edited by Charles Abeysekera and Newton Gunasinghe (Colombo: Social Scientists Association, 1987), pp. 84–85, for further references to the contribution of British scholars to the celebration of Saiva Siddhanta.

**9.** Seneviratne, "South Indian Cultural Nationalism," p. 4.

**10.** P. Sundaram Pillai, *Milestones in the History of Tamil Literature*, cited in Seneviratne, "South Indian Cultural Nationalism," p. 5.

**11.** Seneviratne, "South Indian Cultural Nationalism," p. 11.

**12.** Ibid., p. 8.

**13.** Ibid., p. 13.

**14.** Dagmar Hellmann-Rajanayagam, "The Politics of the Tamil Past," in *Sri Lanka: History and the Roots of Conflict*, p. 118.

**15.** Seneviratne, "South Indian Cultural Nationalism," p. 14.

**16.** S. Pathmanathan, "The Hindu Society in Sri Lanka: Changed and Changing," in *Religiousness in Sri Lanka*, p. 150.

**17.** "[The Sinhalese] gave the Tamils good reason to identify themselves with the Dravidianism of South India when they launched a nationalist revivalist movement of their own in the process of which they embraced the Aryanism of North India. The rhetoric of Sinhalese revivalists like Anagarika Dharmapala and Piyadasa Sirisena totally ignored South India and fixed its gaze on North India. The Sinhalese revivalist movement, in many ways like the Tamil one, posited a pure Sri Lankan Buddhist culture (but related to North India), in the same way as the Tamils harked back to a pure and pristine Tamil culture." Seneviratne, "South Indian Cultural Nationalism," p. 15.

**18.** Ibid.

**19.** "[Navalar's] revival movement was not confined to Sri Lanka only but reached out into South India as well" (Sathasivam, "Hindu Religious Heritage," p. 165). "The philosophy of Saiva Siddhanta became an important part of Tamil identity in Sri Lanka when Arumuga Navalar, the great nineteenth century reformer, revived the doctrine in Jaffna and South India" (Coomaraswamy, "Myths without Conscience," p. 85). Cf. K. M. de Silva, *Managing Ethnic Tensions*, pp. 37–38.

**20.** The phrases are found in Pathmanathan, "Hindu Society in Sri Lanka," p. 153. At the same time, K. M. de Silva points out that the "crucial flaw in Navalar's work . . . was that he was not a social reformer. The Hindu revivalist movement which he led strengthened orthodoxy—as indeed it was intended to—and did little to soften the rigors of the caste system in the Tamil areas of the country. Where the Sinhalese caste system had merely a social sanction the Tamil prototype was deeply embedded in society through the sanctions of Hinduism" (*Managing Ethnic Tensions*, p. 38).

**21.** Sathasivam, "Hindu Religious Heritage," p. 168.

**22.** Ibid.

**23.** Jane Russell, *Communal Politics under the Donoughmore Constitution, 1931–1947* (Dehiwala, Sri Lanka: Tisara Prakasakayo, Ltd., 1983), pp. 110–112. Though Seneviratne does not mention it, this evidence shows that missionaries exerted negative as well as positive influence on the rise of Sri Lankan Tamil nationalism. This should be remembered along with the more positive contributions the missionaries made to the rise of Sri Lankan Tamil nationalism. Cf. K. M. de Silva, *Managing Ethnic Tensions*, p. 37: More or less throughout the nineteenth century, "the missionary organizations were much stronger in Jaffna and its environs than in most other parts of the island. There were fewer sectarian conflicts among the missionaries working in the north, and their network of schools was far more efficiently run. It would appear that the colonial government was less sensitive to potential risks of occasional or general outbursts of popular hostility to missionary activity in the Tamil areas of the country than with the reaction to mission work among the Buddhists."

**24.** Seneviratne, "South Indian Cultural Nationalism," p. 18.

**25.** Ibid., p. 19.

**26.** Ibid.

**27.** Seneviratne does not go into this matter, but it seems directly relevant to his argument. The way the Sri Lankan Tamils go on to defend their claims is reminiscent of South Indian arguments.

**28.** Hellmann-Rajanayagam, "Politics of the Tamil Past," p. 114.

**29.** A statement in 1935, issued by the Federated Communities Progressive Association, a forerunner of the Federal Party, cited in Russell, *Communal Politics*, pp. 147–148.

**30.** A statement published in 1983, but representative of the attitude taking shape in the 1930s, cited in Coomaraswamy, "Myths without Conscience," pp. 82–83.

**31.** Hellmann-Rajanayagam, "Politics of the Tamil Past," p. 115.

**32.** Ibid. Kemper remarks: "If the nagas and yakas that Vijaya encountered were not literally snakes and demons but South Indians, the Tamil claim on Sri Lanka improves proportionally, and this the Sinhala fundamentalist interpretation of the Mahavamsa will not tolerate" (*Presence of the Past*, p. 120).

**33.** Seneviratne, "South Indian Cultural Nationalism," p. 17.

**34.** Ibid., p. 18.

**35.** Ibid., p. 23.

36. Ibid., pp. 15–16.

37. Ibid., p. 16.

38. Ibid., p. 17.

39. Ibid., p. 16

40. Ibid., p. 17.

41. Ibid. Though specific figures are not publicly available.

42. Perinbanayagam, transcript, pp. 14 and 21.

43. Ibid., p. 21.

44. Ibid., p. 14.

45. Ibid., p. 15.

46. Ibid., p. 14.

47. Ibid., pp. 18, 19.

48. Ibid., p. 15. In correspondence, Seneviratne emphasizes his contention that while reaction to the discriminatory practices against the Tamils by the government in the fifties and after is one important cause of Tamil resistance, it cannot fully explain Tamil nationalism, and especially not the separatist movement. Separatism rests on cultural nationalism and a sense of political independence that was in part crucially inspired by South Indian nationalism.

49. Ibid., p. 15.

50. Ibid., p. 15. Perinbanayagam goes on: "In my view, this is the basis of the support of the expatriates for the Tamil cause. These are men and women who came to maturity in the 60s and 70s, and were seeking to build careers in various positions. Many of them therefore experienced the virulence of [communal favoritism by the Sinhala] in their personal lives. Many of them went to universities and . . . were subject to abuse of many kinds, including from their teachers."

51. Ibid., pp. 15–16.

52. Seneviratne appears to embrace that point; see especially p. 37 and n. 4 above, where explicit reference is made to the importance of local Sri Lankan conditions in forming the identity of the Sri Lankan Tamils. In the discussion, C. R. de Silva seemed to say as much: "I tend to accept part of the argument H. L. [Seneviratne] is making, particularly with regard to the earlier period" (transcript, p. 20). Stanley Tambiah (addressing Perinbanayagam) concurred: "The connection [of the Sri Lankan Tamils]

to the Dravidian movement is not as tenuous as you imply. I would like to bring [you and Seneviratne] together. There is a fit here—a [particular] time period—when [the connection] may have been there" (transcript, p. 18). Tambiah emphasizes the special importance of Arumuga Navalar in establishing the distinct cultural connection between South India and the Jaffna Tamil community, a connection, Tambiah says, that even in his own youth continued to be important. Loudspeakers were installed in the public square and "you could hear nothing but ten-hour programs of South Indian music, nationalist songs, and so on. So you may want to reconsider to what extent [these things had an impact]. I completely agree with you that the way the movement has gone now, the LTTE boys and so on may have forged a new ideological justification" (transcript, p. 18). And Vernon Mendis also agrees. He cites the political impact on the 1967 Indian election of the Dravidian movement: "It was a landmark in India. For the first time the mighty colossus of the Congress was shattered." As to the influence of this movement on Sri Lanka, "there was one." It was conveyed by means of the International Association of Tamil Research. It had "a practical impact which drew the politics and culture of Jaffna within the [movement for] Dravidastan." Jaffna was not entirely caught up in the South Indian movement, "but there was an influence." At the same time, Jaffna retained its own identity. Jaffna residents do not see themselves as part of greater South India, but they do incline to establish their own independent place in Sri Lanka (transcript, p. 23). In correspondence, Perinbanayagam rejects Mendis's point about the International Association of Tamil Research. In reality, the association was founded, he says, "purely for research purposes and became political in Mendis's sense only after the persecution of the Tamils became acute." It is not so much the influences from South India but "rampant Sinhala chauvinism" that is important "in alienating the Tamils and driving them towards their present plight."

53. Hellmann-Rajanayagam, "Politics of the Tamil Past," p. 118 (emphasis added). The author goes on to specify the variety of Sri Lankan Tamil responses: "If they chose, their history, unlike Sinhala history, was not bound to Sri Lanka or even to Jaffna; they could, and often did, look towards Tamil Nadu or south India. But this was an option rejected by many in the 1950s in favour of a Sri Lankan past. . . . When this option was repeatedly rejected by the Sinhala between the 1930s and the 1950s, a period of Tamil

introspection began to take shape. This led to the extolling of Tamil virtues over against Sinhala perfidy, to claims for autonomy, and finally independence" (p. 115).

**54.** Coomaraswamy, "Myths without Conscience," pp. 77ff.

**55.** Ibid., pp. 77–78.

## 5. Failure of "Cosmopolitanism"

**1.** The phrase is from *Essays in National Idealism* (1909) by the Tamil leader A. K. Coomaraswamy (cited in Russell, *Communal Politics*, p. 105).

**2.** K. M. de Silva, *Managing Ethnic Tensions*, p. 162.

**3.** Ibid., p. 52.

**4.** Tambiah, *Sri Lanka: Ethnic Fratricide and the Dismantling of Democracy* (Chicago: University of Chicago Press, 1986), pp. 129–131.

**5.** K. M. de Silva, *Managing Ethnic Tensions*, p. 51. Before 1931, the franchise was limited to about 4 percent of Sri Lankan males.

**6.** Ibid., p. 125.

**7.** The Donoughmore Commission recommended the vote for all men over twenty-one and all women over thirty, though this was later amended to include all women over twenty-one.

**8.** Russell, *Communal Politics*, p. 336.

**9.** K. M. de Silva, *Managing Ethnic Tensions*, pp. 103–105. The quotations are from a report by the secretary of state for colonial affairs, written in 1938. The comments made in the Donoughmore Commission Report of 1928 underscore colonial fear of ethnic division: "Not only is the population not homogenous, but the divergent elements of which it is composed distrust and suspect each other. It is almost time to say that the conception of patriotism in Ceylon is as much racial as national and that the best interests of the country are synonymous with the welfare of a particular section of the country" (cited in A. J. Wilson, *The Break-Up of Sri Lanka: The Sinhalese-Tamil Conflict* [London: C. Hurst & Co., 1988], p. 13).

**10.** Tambiah, *Sri Lanka*, p. 109.

**11.** Ibid.

**12.** Russell, *Communal Politics*, pp. 334–335, 341. "Under the Donoughmore Constitution, the Executive System proved to be an effective vehicle for channeling parochial considerations into executive decision-making." (p. 341).

13. Ibid., p. 342: "In Ceylon, it was not the national ideas or character but the communal ideas and the sense of communal identification which increased sharply under the impact of universal franchise."

14. K. M. de Silva, *Managing Ethnic Tensions*, pp. 130–131.

15. Coomaraswamy, *Sri Lanka*, pp. 14–15.

16. Ibid.

17. K. M. de Silva, *Managing Ethnic Tensions*, p. 129. Cf. Coomaraswamy, *Sri Lanka*, pp. 11–12; Coomaraswamy, *Sri Lanka's Ethnic Conflict: Mythology, Power and Politics* (Colombo: International Centre for Ethnic Studies,1984), p. 4.

18. K. M. de Silva, *Managing Ethnic Tensions*, p. 130; Coomaraswamy, *Sri Lanka*, p. 11.

19. Coomaraswamy, *Sri Lanka*, p. 11.

20. K. M. de Silva, *Managing Ethnic Tensions*, p. 129.

21. Coomaraswamy, *Sri Lanka*, pp. 11–12.

22. Rogers, "Regionalism and Ethnicity," expanded comments, p. 8. It ought to be mentioned, though, that not all the Tamil leaders shared this negative attitude toward the Indian Tamils. One of the most important leaders, S. J. V. Chelvanayagam, claimed that the "need for as many Tamils as possible to be on the electoral registers was urgent because, as he [Senanayake] said to me, 'democracy is a matter of numbers.' Those who did not agitate for the re-enfranchisement of the Indian Tamils were therefore 'traitors' who paved the way for the diminution of the Tamils as a political force" (Wilson, *Break-Up of Sri Lanka*, p. 100).

23. K. M. de Silva, *Managing Ethnic Tensions*, p. 155: "On one issue however [Senanayake] shared all prejudices of the Sinhalese politicians (except to Marxists of this period): on the Indian question." Rogers comments that "Sinhalese politicians pictured Indian Tamils . . . as foreign, privileged groups that had thrived at the expense of the Sinhalese peasantry. . . . Previously, relations between Kandyan villagers and Tamils had been good although not close, but in the midst of the rural hardship brought on by the depression it was easy to make the Tamils into scapegoats. . . . Indian Tamils were denied many of the benefits of legislation passed in the 1930s and 1940s, especially those concerned with land policy, and shortly

after Independence they were deprived, with the connivance of the Ceylon Tamil leadership, of both their voting rights and their citizenship" ("Social Mobility," p. 594).

According to de Silva, there were additional motivations for neutralizing the Indian Tamil vote. Left-wing parties derived considerable support from the Indian Tamils, and by disenfranchising them the UNP strengthened its position (*Managing Ethnic Tensions*, p. 155). Interestingly enough, the Marxists and left-wing party members criticized this legislation as overtly racist. See Ram, *Sri Lanka: The Fractured Island*, p. 37.

**24.** Coomaraswamy, *Sri Lanka*, p. 11.

**25.** Seneviratne emphasizes in correspondence that Senenayake's motivation for disenfranchising the Indian Tamils was political fear of the Marxists who were busy at the time trying to mobilize the Indian Tamils. According to Seneviratne, he was "actually obsessed with a fear of the Marxists." Nina Samarasinghe provides supporting evidence for this conclusion in her 1989 Oxford Ph.D. dissertation, "Colonial Policy, Ethnic Politics and the Minorities in Ceylon (Sri Lanka), 1927–1947": "D. S. Senanayake is reported to have warned the Sinhalese that in the event of gaining power, the Communist Party would distribute land to the Indians.... 'Let not an exotic ideology corrupt our body politic and disrupt its members [he wrote]. Let us keep our national character unsullied by these foreign contaminating influences'" (p. 320).

At the same time, it must not be forgotten, as Samarasinghe also shows, that in combatting the Marxists, Senanayake and other UNP leaders explicitly played on Sinhala Buddhist nationalist sentiments, even though such a maneuver contradicted the UNP's cosmopolitian image. "Everything the UNP stood for, traditional values, religion and policies were presented to the voters as being threatened by the Marxist Left. In spite of the UNP stand as a secular and non-ethnic party, it appealed to the primordial ethnic identity of the voter. It called out to the quality of the voter as a Sinhalese, Tamil, Muslim, Buddhist or Hindu" (p. 320).

Interesting, too, was Senanayake's anti-modernism. "In the name of the ancient spirituality of the east, the UNP offered the vision of a new nation closed to the outer world and to progress. Modernisation was synonymous with 'immoral promiscuous living.' Senanayake was totally hostile to 'the transformation of the proud independent peasant'.... Instead the UNP candidates pledged to protect what they perceived as the 'national character.' By so doing what they enhanced were in fact the values of the predominantly agrarian Sinhalese society. . . . The national identity that was projected was an idealized perception of Sinhalese ethnicity" (p. 321).

**26.** Kemper, *Presence of the Past*, p. 161.

**27.** Ibid., pp. 66–69.

**28.** Ibid., p. 162.

**29.** Ibid. In the late 1930s, Senanayake was energetically championing Sinhala Buddhist communal interests. "He warned of the need for solidarity to protect the 'race' and the Buddhist faith. He sometimes equated the 'nation' with the Sinhalese population, speaking of them as 'one blood, and one nation . . . a chosen people.' He favoured a ban on the sale of land to non-Ceylonese, spoke of the Indians' 'treacherous' love of their own land, and endorsed the disenfranchisement of Indian workers with comments such as this: 'I do not think a greater blow to the national life of a country has been dealt, even by the Germans in Poland, than what has been done Up-country by the enfranchisement of so many Indian labourers'" (James Manor, *The Expedient Utopian: Bandaranaike and Ceylon* [Cambridge: Cambridge University Press, 1989], p. 133).

**30.** Kemper, *Presence of the Past*, pp. 161–162, as a description of Senanayake's attitude uttered by John Kotelawala. Kotelawala would succeed Senanayake's son, Dudley, as prime minister and serve until 1956. Dudley Senanayake became prime minister upon the death of his father in 1952.

**31.** Patrick Peebles, "Colonization and Ethnic Conflict in the Dry Zone of Sri Lanka," *Journal of Asian Studies* 49, 1 (February 1990): 37.

**32.** Ibid. The phrase "millennial visions" is drawn from an article by G. H. Peiris, "Agrarian Transformations in British Sri Lanka," cited in Peebles (n. 34 below).

**33.** *Ceylon Daily News*, April 17, 1939, cited in Jayawardena, *Ethnic and Class Conflicts*, p. 53.

**34.** Peebles, "The Accelerated Mahaweli Programme and Ethnic Conflict," paper presented to the working group conference, p. 3, citing Mick Moore, *The State and Peasant Politics in Sri Lanka* (Cambridge: Cambridge University Press, 1985), p. 45.

**35.** Whether the colonization program begun under Senanayake, and later expanded into the Accelerated Mahaweli Program, was in fact unfair and discriminatory toward Tamils is a hotly controversial question to which we shall return later.

**36.** K. M. de Silva, *Managing Ethnic Tensions*, p. 215.

**37.** Wilson, *Break-Up of Sri Lanka*, p. 93.

**38.** K. M. de Silva, *Managing Ethnic Tensions*, p. 156.

**39.** "On the eve of independence few men in power had perceived or were willing to perceive the complex nature of the Ceylonese polity (and the true meaning of democracy).... The minorities would, it was thought, accommodate to a measured Sinhalese majority domination over the country. British officials shared the same delusion. Looking back on those years, it seems unimaginable that the forces of ethnicity, both Sinhalese and Tamil, and the absence of any overriding national feeling did not then strike policy makers and lead them to reassess the adequacy of implanting the Westminster model in Ceylon.... By denying the principle of ethnicity in politics as contradictory to modernisation while at the same time practicing ethnic politics through majoritarian rule, Sinhalese politicians of the 1930s and 1940s paved the way for the emergence of what has been called the Sinhalese Buddhist revolution of S. W. R. D. Bandaranaike. It can be demonstrated from the findings of this book that the break or turning point of 1956 was inherent in the Sinhalese reconquest which started much earlier, in 1931 with the institution of democratic politics." Samarasinghe, "Colonial Policy," pp. 341–342.

**40.** Kemper, *Presence of the Past*, p. 163.

**41.** Tambiah, *Sri Lanka*, p. 132.

**42.** Manor, *Expedient Utopian*, p. 69: Like his father and relatives, Bandaranaike regarded the Senanayakes as nouveau riche and of lower estate. The feeling was mutual. Senanayake took great offense that Bandaranaike's maternal grandfather blamed the ethnic riots of 1915 on Senanayake and his friends for trying "to pose as leaders of the Buddhists ... nobodies [hoping] to make somebodies of themselves."

**43.** Ibid., p. 31.

**44.** Ibid., p. 52.

**45.** "A New Era," 1926, cited in Russell, *Communal Politics*, p. 328.

**46.** Manor, *Expedient Utopian*, p. 112: "It could not have escaped a man as preoccupied with politics as Bandaranaike that the change made good political sense. There can be no doubt that this influenced his decision and that some of his explanations for the change are rationalizations. But these explanations also contain enough substance and coherence to suggest that this was, to a very considerable extent, an honest decision."

47. Ibid., p. 115.

48. Ibid., p. 114.

49. Kemper, *Presence of the Past*, p. 164.

50. Amunugama, "S. W. R. D. Bandaranaike and the Buddhist Monks," forthcoming, p. 8. I am grateful to Mr. Amunugama for giving me access to this enlightening discussion of the political sources of Bandaranaike's chauvinism.

51. Ibid., p. 5.

52. Ibid.

53. Ibid., p. 3. Amunugama disputes Manor's claim that "pressure by Sinhalese cultural revivalists from the literary world forced the adoption of a largely communalist set of aims" (Manor, *Expedient Utopian*, p. 128). "To those familiar with Bandaranaike's penchant for drafting memoranda and constitutions, this description of the founding of the Sinhala Maha Sabha must appear to be most dubious. . . . The fact that Bandaranaike based his campaigns on the SMS platform, and in fact intensified the nationalist component of it, clearly indicates that he was behind the original charter of the Sinhala Maha Sabha" (Amunugama, "S. W. R. D. Bandaranaike," p. 3).

54. Russell, *Communal Politics*, pp. 145–146.

55. K. M. de Silva, *Managing Ethnic Tensions*, p. 125.

56. Cited in Russell, *Communal Politics*, p. 146.

57. Cited in Manor, *Expedient Utopian*, p. 130.

58. Ibid.

59. Russell, *Communal Politics*, p. 146.

60. R. C. Kanangara, remarks made in 1936, cited in ibid., pp. 151–152.

61. R. Sri Pathmanathan, cited in ibid., p. 149.

62. Tambiah, *Buddhism Betrayed?* especially chaps. 4–6.

63. "Dharmapala . . . set in motion a significant political trend by inducting young Sinhala Bhikkhus for missionary activity in India. Several such monks, who were trained in Bengal, were fascinated by revolutionary politics in the province and the struggle

for Indian independence" (Amunugama, "Buddhaputra and Bhumiputra?" pp. 10–11).

**64.** Ibid., p. 15, n. 1. Another consequence of Dharmapala's association with India was that the "Vidyalankara Pirivena . . . established strong links" there. Still again, Dharmapala was responsible for establishing a department of Pali studies at the University of Calcutta, where several Sinhala scholar monks went to teach (ibid., p. 11).

**65.** Ibid., p. 11.

**66.** Tambiah, *Buddhism Betrayed?* p. 17. Cf. Amunugama, "Buddhaputra and Bhumiputra?" p. 17.

**67.** Tambiah, *Buddhism Betrayed?* p. 19.

**68.** Ibid., p. 20.

**69.** Amunugama, "Buddhaputra and Bhumiputra?" p. 18.

**70.** K. M. de Silva, "Buddhist Revivalism," p. 135.

**71.** Ibid., p. 17.

**72.** Ibid.

**73.** Walpola Rahula, *The Heritage of the Bhikku: A Short History of the Bhikku in the Educational, Cultural, Social, and Political Life* (New York: Grove Press, 1974). D. C. Vijayawardena, *Dharma-Vijaya, or The Revolt in the Temple* (Colombo: Sinha Publications, 1953). *The Betrayal of Buddhism: An Abridged Version of the Report by the Buddhist Committee of Enquiry* (Balangoda: Dharmavijaya Press, 1956).

**74.** Cited in Tambiah, *Buddhism Betrayed?* p. 26. Cf. the discussion of Rahula by K. M. de Silva, "Buddhist Revivalism," pp. 128–31, and Bond, *Buddhist Revival*, pp. 69–70.

**75.** Tambiah, *Buddhism Betrayed?* p. 28 (emphasis added).

**76.** Ibid.

**77.** Ibid., p. 38.

**78.** Cited in ibid., pp. 38–39 (Tambiah's emphasis).

**79.** Cited in Bond, *Buddhist Revival*, p. 85.

**80.** Tambiah, *Buddhism Betrayed?* p. 35.

**81.** Bond, *Buddhist Revival*, p. 88.

**82.** K. M. de Silva, *Managing Ethnic Conflict*, pp. 176, 177.

**83.** Bond, correspondence.

**84.** Tambiah, *Buddhism Betrayed?* pp. 44–45.

## 6. Full Circle

1. *Economist*, December 5, 1992.

2. Cited in ibid.

3. Tambiah, *Sri Lanka*, p. 71.

4. Issued on July 26, 1957, by Prime Minister Bandaranaike and "representatives of the Federal Party [including Chelvanayagam]." See app. 1, Rohan Gunaratna, *War and Peace in Sri Lanka* (Colombo: Institute of Fundamental Studies, 1987), pp. 74–75.

5. Ibid., pp. 71–73, and K. M. de Silva, *Managing Ethnic Conflict*, pp. 186–187.

6. Manor, *Expedient Utopian*, p. 256.

7. K. M. de Silva, *Managing Ethnic Tensions*, p. 182: Bandaranaike "was to find that the past—his own past, in particular—was often a hostage to the future and *vice versa.*"

8. The term is K. M. de Silva's. See especially chap. 13, "Linguistic Nationalism and Buddhist Resurgence, 1956–1972," and chap. 14, "Linguistic Nationalism, the Tamil Version, 1948–1972," in *Managing Ethnic Tensions*, pp. 196–226.

9. "To the Sinhalese, the linkage between language and religion was central to the assertion of ethnic identity" (ibid., p. 216). Even though, as de Silva points out, religion and language were "not as organically linked" for the Tamils, still the fact that the two were so closely connected in the Sinhala case inevitably meant that the religious dimension of the linguistic dispute was an important part of the ethnic conflict.

10. Ibid., p. 217.

11. Reggie Siriwardena, "National Identity in Sri Lanka: Problems in Communication and Education," in *Sri Lanka—The Ethnic Conflict: Myths, Realities and Perspectives* (New Delhi: Navrang, 1984), p. 218. Siriwardena highlights the Aryan-Dravidian "racial" distinctions that are part of the Sinhala ideology, and he singles out Anagarika Dharmapala as "a particularly strident example of Aryan myth-making" (pp. 218–219).

12. Ibid., p. 216.

13. "The power of the language issue lay in the fact that it combined a central ideological tenet of cultural nationalism—the purity of the Sinhala language (and race) and its role in maintaining and defending Buddhism—with an economic appeal that blamed

the present-day weakness of the Sinhalese on the second-rate status
of Sinhala. Although there was little difference in the overall wealth
of most Sinhalese and Ceylon Tamils, Sinhalese propagandists pointed
to the fact that the smaller ethnic group accounted for a disproportionate share of jobs in the professions and the middle and
upper levels of government administration. *Here was an issue ready-
made for exploitation by politicians seeking electoral advantage, but as
in the years before 1915, although on a much greater scale, they soon
lost control of the emotions they helped to create"* (Rogers, "Social
Mobility," p. 595, emphasis added). Cf. Tambiah, *Sri Lanka*, pp.
73–77; Ram, *Sri Lanka: The Fractured Island*, pp. 39–41.

"The Bandaranaike administration enacted the Official Language
Act of 1956 making Sinhalese the only official language replacing
English [as, in effect, a policy of affirmative action for the Sinhalese].
There was widespread support for the move from the Sinhalese
but strong opposition from the Tamils. The change had both substantive and symbolic significance. At the symbolic level it signalled
the triumph of Sinhalese nationalism. At the substantive level, from
a national perspective, it had both advantages as well as disadvantages. Proficiency in English was limited to a small urban elite
probably no more than 10% to 15% of the population. Therefore,
conducting government business in a language that was undestood
by the common people was a progressive step. . . . The policy also
had its drawbacks. It sharply divided the country along ethnic
lines. The Tamils felt alienated. . . .

"Language is a key element of the ethnic identity of both Sinhalese and Tamils. However, language policy also had other practical implications in areas such as jobs and education. The [affirm-
ative action] element in Sri Lanka's official policy stems from that.
When government business began to be conducted in Sinhalese,
inevitably, more jobs in government became available to the Sinhalese. Provision was made for Tamils to join government service
without proficiency in Sinhalese. However, they were required to
pass a Sinhalese language examination within a prescribed time
period. Otherwise they were denied promotion, salary increments
and eventually faced the threat of dismissal. . . .

"The impact of this policy was seen, for example, in the recruitment to the general clerical service of the central government. In
1949, when English was the official language, 54% of the recruits
were Sinhalese and 41% Tamils. In 1955 the year before Sinhalese
was made the official language the shares of the two communities

were 66% and 39% respectively. In 1963 the figures were 92% and 7% respectively. Two points are worth noting here. There was a significant increase in the Sinhalese share and a parallel decrease in the Tamil share even before 1956. Thus, the language policy alone could not have been responsible for the change. Second, after 1956 there had been a precipitous drop in Tamil recruitment which was associated with, and probably caused by, the language policy. ... " S. W. R. de A. Samarasinghe, "Affirmative Action and Equity in Multiethnic Societies: The Sri Lankan Experience," in *Affirmative Action: The International Experience* (Johannesburg, South Africa: Urban Foundation, forthcoming), pp. 4–5 (unpublished version).

In a phone conversation (July 22, 1993), Mr. Samarasinghe emphasized his view that the language policy of 1956, together with later policies in the 1970s, distinctly "exacerbated" the ethnic problem. However justified a policy of affirmative action in favor of the Sinhalese may have been, the government was insensitive and inattentive to the devastating consequences of the policy on the Tamils, and thus was responsible to an important extent for the worsening ethnic relations that resulted. See pp. 145–146 for further elaboration of the discriminatory aspects of government policy.

14. Manor, *Expedient Utopian*, p. 262.

15. Ibid.

16. Ibid., p. 268.

17. Ibid., p. 270.

18. Tambiah, *Buddhism Betrayed?* p. 48.

19. Manor, *Expedient Utopian*, pp. 291–292.

20. K. M. de Silva, *Managing Ethnic Tensions*, p. 199.

21. Ibid., pp. 201–202.

22. Vernon Mendis, interview, United States Institute of Peace, Washington, D.C., December 22, 1992.

23. K. M. de Silva, *Managing Ethnic Tensions*, p. 527.

24. Ibid.

25. Ibid., p. 271.

26. Ibid., p. 202.

27. Despite Dudley Senanayake's denunciation of the Bandaranaike-Chelvanayagam pact of 1957, his inclination toward moderation triumphed in his willingness to reach a new accord with Chelvanayagam on March 24, 1965. Like the earlier pact, the

Senanayake-Chelvanayagam pact conceded the use of Tamil as the administrative language in the northern and eastern provinces, provided for a degree of local political control in the form of district councils (the earlier pact had regional councils), and reserved "the granting of land under colonisation schemes," according to the following three priorities: "(A) Land in the Northern and Eastern Provinces should in the first instance be granted to landless people in the District; (B) Secondly to Tamil speaking persons resident in the Northern and Eastern Provinces; and (C) Thirdly to other citizens in Ceylon, preference being given to Tamil citizens in the rest of the Island" (app. 2, Gunaratna, *War and Peace*, p. 76).

**28.** Horowitz, "Making Moderation Pay," p. 462.

**29.** Ibid. How discriminatory government policy actually was is a disputed point. Vernon Mendis writes in correspondence: "The quota system may not have been the ideal solution but the object was to give the Sinhala who are the majority community their proportionately rightful share of employment. The Tamil propaganda on this betrays a feeling of selfishness and disregard for the rights and aspirations of others. [The quota system] cannot be called religious or cultural chauvinism but legitimate steps to protect the interests of the majority community. The actual measures could have been worked out more carefully to ensure that they were fair and equitable but the need for them cannot be questioned. . . . Though the proportions [of Tamils] may have fallen there was no real erosion of the numbers of Tamils holding positions and this continues to be the position today."

But for a contrasting and (to the author) more persuasive account, see S. W. R. de A. Samarasinghe, "Ethnic Representation in Central Government Employment and Sinhala-Tamil Relations in Sri Lanka, 1948–1981," in *From Independence to Statehood*, edited by Robert B. Goldman and A. Jeyaratnam Wilson (London: Frances Pinter, 1984), pp. 173–184: "Recently influential Tamil opinion in Sri Lanka has repeatedly focused attention on 'discrimination against Tamils in government employment.' The basis of this complaint is the relatively low level of recruitment of Tamils in recent years to certain grades in government service. For example, Table 4 shows that Tamil recruitment to the General Clerical service has fallen sharply since the early 1960s. The table also shows that less than 5% of a recent group of police recruits were Tamils and that only 6.1% of the teachers recruited in 1977–79 were Tamils. Table 5 shows that Tamil recruitment to the Administrative Service has also fallen in recent years. Several other similar examples were highlighted in recent parliamentary discussions on the question; in most instances cited, Tamil recruitment has fallen to less than 10% of the total. . . .

"Given the fact that governments in Sri Lanka have increasingly come to be guided by electoral considerations in their conduct of business it is not surprising that awarding jobs to one's own voters (mostly Sinhalese) takes precedence. The importance governments attach to this level of political patronage is evidenced by the fact that over the past decade or so, in several instances, relatively impartial systems of recruitment through examination and interview have been abandoned in favour of an interview alone or simply a recommendation by a member of Parliament" (pp. 180–181). See also C. R. de Silva, "The Politics of University Admissions: A Review of Some Aspects of the Admissions Policy in Sri Lanka, 1971–1978," *Sri Lanka Journal of Social Sciences* I, 2: 85–132. Cf. n. 13, above, and n. 32, below.

30. K. M. de Silva, *Managing Ethnic Tensions*, p. 262.

31. *Inter-Racial Equity and National Unity in Sri Lanka* (Colombo: Marga Institute, 1985), p. 22. This is a report that, in general, tends to regard many of the allegations of discrimination against the Tamils in such things as education, employment, and land distribution as somewhat exaggerated.

32. K. M. de Silva, *Managing Ethnic Tensions*, p. 311.

33. C. R. de Silva, "Weightage in University Admissions: Standardization and District Quotas in Sri Lanka," *Modern Ceylon Studies* 5, 2: 166, cited by K. M. de Silva, *Managing Ethnic Tensions*, p. 266. K. M. de Silva remarks: "For the Tamils the district quota system was a heavy blow: the percentage of university places in the science-based disciplines held by them fell from 35.3% in 1970 to 20.9% in 1974 and 19% in 1975. In 1974 there was, for the first time, a substantial fall in the absolute number of Tamils entering the science-based courses despite a continued expansion in the total intake in those courses" (p. 266). He continues: "The Sinhalese . . . profited enormously from this [education policy] even if those resident in Colombo, and to a lesser extent in other urban areas, suffered a drop in the number of admissions too; in science-based courses they now constituted 75.5% in 1974; and this figure rose, even higher to 78.0% in 1975. Since they had over 86% of the

places in the humanities and social sciences, *Sinhalese students were now in the same privileged position in the universities as their politicians were in the national legislature in terms of seats there.* The Moors/ Malays saw their number of admissions to science-based courses double between 1970 and 1975, even though they were still well below the magic figure of 6–7%, the ethnic quota which some of their political leaders advocated as their due" (p. 266, emphasis added).

**34.** K. M. de Silva, *Managing Ethnic Tensions*, pp. 253–254, though the constitution had little to do with the accommodation. It had more to do with a change of heart on both sides, politically motivated on the part of Mrs. Bandaranaike, and motivated by a more liberal outlook in connection with Vatican II on the part of the Roman Catholics.

**35.** Coomaraswamy, *Sri Lanka*, p. 22.

**36.** Ibid., p. 31.

**37.** Ibid., p. 29.

**38.** K. M. de Silva, *Managing Ethnic Tensions*, p. 256.

**39.** Rogers, "Regionalism and Ethnicity," p. 13.

**40.** K. M. de Silva, *Managing Ethnic Tensions*, pp. 257–258.

**41.** Cited in K. M. de Silva, *Managing Ethnic Conflicts*, p. 259.

**42.** Ibid., pp. 260–261.

**43.** See above, chap. 4, "The Tamil Response," especially pp. 42–43.

**44.** Rogers, "Regionalism and Ethnicity," p. 15.

**45.** Kemper, *Presence of the Past*, p. 127. "President Jayewardene had a reputation as a hardliner on the ethnic issue. A student of archeology, passionately involved in Buddhist historical research, and *a former office bearer of the Anagarika Dharmapala Trust*, he was very sympathetic to the Buddhist view" (Amunugama, "Buddhaputra and Bhumiputra?" p. 6, emphasis added).

**46.** Coomaraswamy, *Sri Lanka*, p. 40.

**47.** Kemper, *Presence of the Past*, p. 171: "His enemies frequently pointed out that there was also something unmistakable about the monarchist imagery of Jayewardene's administration. One of the complaints people made most often about Jayewardene was his pretension. After his election, he asked people to address him by the honorific *utumananuvahanse* (Your Excellency), a considerable elevation in the protocol of high office. . . . Describing himself as the inheritor to the Sri Lankan monarchy, Jayewardene made speeches that sounded eerily similar to arguments Sri Lankan kings are known to have made."

48. Coomaraswamy, *Sri Lanka*, pp. 41, 45. See chap. 3, "Trimming the Sails: The Gaullist Constitution of 1978."

49. Buddhist teaching, or Buddhism as a historical phenomenon.

50. *Nava Mavatak* (*A New Path*), collected speeches of J. R. Jayewardene (1978), cited in Kemper, *Presence of the Past*, pp. 173–174.

51. The following distinction between what is actually known about Asoka's kingdom and certain unverified legends about it that later came to be embraced by South Asian Buddhists was proposed by Stanley Tambiah in correspondence: "The principle evidence on Emperor Asoka's rule is provided by the Rock Edicts. These convey that while Asoka was a Buddhist himself, he and his queens were liberal in their support of the adherents of all faiths—Buddhists, Jains, Brahmins, and Ajivikas. His conception of benevolent kingship based on *dharma* was principally inspired by Buddhist values. It is however the Buddhist (mythohistorical) chronicles of *later times*, such as the *Mahavamsa* . . . and the *Asokavandana* (a Northeast Indian Hinayanist text of around the second century AD), that propagate the idea that the Asokan empire was a Buddhist regime, that Asoka built 84,000 *stupas* containing Buddha's relics all over India, that he made several munificent gifts to Buddhist monks, that he sent Buddhist missions to propagate the faith, and that he set the precedent that Kingship and the Buddhist Sangha, as mutually supporting institutions, are the twin pillars of Buddhist kingdoms. The last thesis in particular is a charter proclaimed in the Buddhist chronicles of Sri Lanka, Thailand, and Burma, and cannot be attributed to his Rock Edicts or any evidence that can be dated to this time" (Tambiah's emphasis).

52. Kemper, "J. R. Jayewardene," p. 192.

53. Kemper, *Presence of the Past*, p. 177.

54. Ibid., p. 200.

55. Ibid., p. 198.

56. Ibid., pp. 197–198.

57. Ibid., pp. 199–200.

58. Ibid., p. 175.

**59.** "Dharmistha Society Cannot Be Built through Legislation—President," *Daily News* (Colombo), January 10, 1980, cited in ibid., p. 176.

**60.** See pp. 56–58, above.

**61.** Peebles, "Accelerated Mahaweli Programme," pp. 4–5: "In 1977 and 1978 the UNP gave the the clear impression that it would implement the entire 30-year development plan proposed in 1968 in six years. On October 27, 1977, Jayewardene told the nation 'our Government has decided to complete all three phases ... in six years.' The project was scaled down several times and when it was completed this year [1990], it included four major dams, and a fifth dam for hydroelectric power, with an installed capacity of 400 megawatts. It plans to irrigate an estimated 390,000 acres of new lands, most of them in the Eastern Province in the Mahaweli and adjacent Madura Oy basins, on which 140,000 families would settle."

**62.** Some of the scholars participating in the conference took different sides. Patrick Peebles stood firmly with those who see colonization as an extension of Sinhala chauvinism. Sarath Amunugama, for one, opposed that view. Other participants stood at various points in between, as we shall see. Beyond the conference, Peebles's position (and a similar position taken by Amita Shastri) has been sharply contested by G. H. Peiris in an unpublished article, "Towards a Better Understanding of the Ethnic Conflict of Sri Lanka: A Response to Two Recent Writings" (which Professor Peiris very kindly made available to me).

**63.** Cited in K. M. de Silva, *Managing Ethnic Conflicts*, p. 260.

**64.** Coomaraswamy, "Myths without Conscience," p. 93.

**65.** C. R. de Silva, transcript, p. 49. In the discussion, Stanley Tambiah emphasized this matter of the perception of discrimination, whatever the intentions of the government may have been. "It is not [by design] inherently anti-Tamil, but the consequences [have the effect of] exclusion" (transcript, p. 53).

**66.** Peebles, "Colonization and Ethnic Conflict," p. 41. Peebles marshals considerable statistical evidence for his conclusion that government colonization policies display a consistent and deliberate pattern of ethnic reconstitution, particularly in the eastern section of the country. For example: "The Sinhalese population of the Eastern Dry Zone increased about five times from 1946 to 1959, and nearly doubled from 1959 to 1976, a tenfold increase in thirty years. The change in the distribution of the population is even greater; from 1946 to 1959 Sinhalese had increased from 19.2 percent to 54.4 percent. In 1976, they were 83.4 percent of the population." Peebles's figures show an increase in the Sinhala population in the eastern dry zone, but they do not prove that the government intended such a result. Sarath Amunugama argued in the conference that Tamils were disinclined to settle in that area.

67. Peiris, "Towards a Better Understanding of the Ethnic Conflict," p. 27.

68. *Inter-Racial Equity*, pp. 39–40.

69. Peiris, "An Appraisal of the Concept of a Traditional Tamil Homeland in Sri Lanka," *Ethnic Studies Report* 9, 1 (January 1991): 13–39; K. M. de Silva, *The "Traditional Homelands" of the Tamils of Sri Lanka: An Historical Appraisal* (Colombo: International Centre for Ethnic Studies, 1987). See also K. M. de Silva, *Managing Ethnic Tensions*, pp. 260–261: "There is little or no evidence to support the claim made in the Vaddukoddai resolution and the TULF manifesto of 1977 that there was either an unbroken 'national' consciousness or a continuing tradition of independent statehood."

70. Peiris, "Appraisal of the Concept of a Traditional Tamil Homeland," p. 34: "The Northern and Eastern Provinces which constitute about 29% of the total area of Sri Lanka are inhabited by 72.6% of the Sri Lankan Tamil population. This latter is equivalent to approximately 9% of the total population of the country. In a densely peopled country like Sri Lanka, where the prevailing pressure of population on land is intense, 9% of its population claiming exclusive rights over 29% of its territory is in itself somewhat unfair. Moreover, the acute scarcity of resources for agriculture from which Sri Lanka suffers implies that the country cannot afford to have uninhabited 'buffer zones' between concentrations of different ethnic groups. Nor can such uninhabited or underutilized tracts of territory be reserved untouched as future lebensraum for any one ethnic group of the country."

71. Amunugama, transcript, pp. 51–52.

72. Ibid.

73. Ibid.

74. Peiris, "Towards a Better Understanding of the Ethnic Conflict," p. 16.

75. *Inter-Racial Equity*, p. 40.

**76.** C. R. de Silva, transcript, p. 50. Professor Peiris emphasizes that nothing he says is meant to "condone inequity in the distribution of the benefits of development . . . [nor to] deny that the so-called 'Indian Tamils' . . . have hitherto been by-passed in the distribution of the benefits of colonization" ("Towards a Better Understanding of the Ethnic Conflict," p. 12).

**77.** *Inter-Racial Equity*, p. 42. I am inferring this consensus inter alia from the conference discussion and from remarks made to me in interviews conducted in Sri Lanka and in the United States.

**78.** "The problem of colonisation is a modern problem of ethnic minorities who are alienated from a state which reflects the interests of a seemingly hostile majority" (Coomaraswamy, "Myths without Conscience," p. 93).

**79.** Perhaps Peebles's account would be strengthened by acknowledging and taking up in detail the government's own justifications for the AMP.

**80.** Peebles, "Accelerated Mahaweli Programme," p. 10, citing words from President Jayewardene himself, and from a Ministry of Plan Implementation document.

**81.** Sorting out the government's motives would be an important area for further investigation. That the Jayewardene government did emphasize Buddhist nationalist themes (albeit in a mode different from predecessors) needs to be borne in mind, though it is hard to know precisely how much weight to ascribe to these themes in directing the AMP.

**82.** See Coomaraswamy, "Myths without Conscience," for an incisive discussion of the dangers of introducing ethnic myths into disputes over land: "All claims to promised land always lead to ethnic chauvinism and a desire for territorial expansion" (p. 97).

**83.** Rogers, "Regionalism and Ethnicity," pp. 15–16.

**84.** K. M. de Silva, *Managing Ethnic Tensions*, p. 315: "In retrospect it would appear that the swift passage of the bill through parliament, and the wide support it received within the UNP constituted a major political achievement. Twice before, once in 1957–58 and again in 1966–68, political initiatives for decentralization of administration had been abandoned in the face of extra-parliamentary agitation and internal bickering within the ranks of the ruling party. On this present occasion not only was the political will to pursue this bill to its eventual enactment altogether greater, the opposition was also altogether weaker and less organized." De Silva continues that the proposal of district councils marked an important departure "from the policy of concentrating administrative and political authorities in Colombo which had been a feature of government policy since independence" (p. 313). In the initial stages, the councils "appeared to have blunted the edges of the [Tamil] separatist agitation, and, indeed, helped to give the restive Jaffna peninsula a brief period of peace" (p. 316).

85. Rogers, "Regionalism and Ethnicity, p. 17.

86. K. M. de Silva, *Managing Ethnic Tensions*, pp. 317–318.

87. Rogers, "Regionalism and Ethnicity," p. 17.

88. See Sieghart, *Sri Lanka*, pp. 29–41, especially p. 33: The "provisions [of the PTA] are quite extraordinarily wide. No legislation conferring even remotely comparable powers is in force in any other free democracy operating under the Rule of Law, however troubled it may be by political . . . violence." Cf. Virginia Leery, *Ethnic Conflict and Violence in Sri Lanka* (International Commission of Jurists and Justice, 1981).

89. Cyril Mathew, in parliamentary debate, June 10, 1981, cited in Coomaraswamy, *Sri Lanka*, p. 73.

90. Ibid., pp. 39–41.

91. Ibid., pp. 30–31.

92. Ibid., p. 30.

93. Rogers, "Regionalism and Ethnicity," p. 16.

94. Ibid., p. 17.

95. Ibid.

96. Kemper, "J. R. Jayewardene," p. 201.

97. Text of Jayewardene's address from *Daily News* (Colombo), July 29, 1983, p. 1, cited in Hurst Hanum, *Autonomy, Sovereignty, and Self-Determination: The Accommodation of Conficting Rights* (Philadelphia: University of Pennsylvania Press, 1990), p. 286.

98. Elizabeth Nissan, "Some Thoughts on Sinhalese Justifications for the Violence [in 1983]," in *Sri Lanka: In Change and Crisis* (New York: St. Martin's Press, 1984), pp. 176–177.

99. Ibid., p. 177.

100. Ibid., p. 176.

101. Sieghart, *Sri Lanka*, p. 42.

102. Ibid., p. 61.

103. Rogers, "Regionalism and Ethnicity," p. 19.

104. Amunugama, "Buddhaputra and Bhumiputra?" p. 1.

105. See Ram, *Sri Lanka: The Fractured Island*, pp. 96–97.

106. Rogers, "Regionalism and Ethnicity," pp. 20–21.

107. Amunugama, "Buddhaputra and Bhumiputra?" pp. 18–19. H. L. Seneviratne adds in correspondence: "Jayewardene downgraded the social role of monks also because these monks came from the marxist tradition. . . . He is somewhat to the right of Ronald Reagan and Adam Smith. He was thrilled that Margaret Thatcher presided ceremonially upon the completion of the AMP."

108. Ibid., p. 23: "The present threat [was] perceived from young Catholic priests who are adherents of 'Liberation Theology.' They live with the poor and in the pursuit of their congregational tasks become a direct rival of the socially oriented monk."

109. Ibid., p. 22: "These fears were compounded when publicity was given in Sinhala media to the involvement of the Catholic Church which provided shelter to the guerrillas, operating in Catholic dominated areas like Mannar."

110. Amunugama admitted it as a "defect" of his paper that he did not treat at greater length the monks who favored the accords. There were several groups, such as those associated with the parties of the left, but nevertheless allied with the UNP. They came out in public support of the accords, and many of them "have a track record of fighting for the minorities and looking after them" and articulating their rights. There were also Sarvodaya monks, as well as the "monks of the frontier," many of whom had Tamil or partly Tamil constituencies and themselves spoke Tamil. Nevertheless, they were not mainstream (transcript, p. 41); "they were small in number and influence" ("Buddhaputra and Bhumiputra?" p. 24).

111. Amunugama, "Buddhaputra and Bhumiputra?" p. 21.

112. See Tambiah, *Buddhism Betrayed?* pp. 80–101.

113. *Vinivida* 14 (June 1988), cited in Amunugama, "Buddhaputra and Bhumiputra?" p. 25: "Those who fight for barren earth are nothing but savages. . . . King Asoka chose Dharma Vijaya because he realized the futility of fighting for land. It being so, we are compelled to characterize those who do not live together but quibble about historic homelands and thereby break up their motherland, as well as those who encourage them, as savages."

114. Amunugama, "Buddhaputra and Bhumiputra?" p. 24.

115. Ibid., pp. 20–21.

116. Ibid., pp. 40–41.

117. Ibid., p. 41.

118. Tambiah, *Buddhism Betrayed?* p. 94.

119. Amunugama, "Buddhaputra and Bhumiputra?" p. 42.

120. As the result of his current work on contemporary developments among Buddhist monks, H. L. Seneviratne mentions in correspondence that "there are young monks in the universities who represent a clear change from the 1956 types. They talk about the uses of English, Western secular knowledge and serving the people in areas that matter, such as poverty alleviation and environmental education, a far cry from the substance-less ideologies of the 1956 era." Some of the monks have gone so far as to advocate substantial concessions to the Tamils in the interest of achieving ethnic harmony.

121. S. W. R. de A. Samarasinghe and Kamala Liyanage, "Friends and Foes of the Indo–Sri Lankan Accord," in *Peace Accords and Ethnic Conflict,* edited by K. M. de Silva and S. W. R. de A. Samarasinghe (London: St. Martin's Press, 1993), p. 170.

122. Ibid.

123. K. M. de Silva, *India in Sri Lanka, 1983–1991,* Woodrow Wilson Center Asia Program Occasional Paper no. 45 (Washington, D.C., February 5, 1992), p. 18.

124. Edward A. Gargan, "Sri Lanka Army Makes Gains against Rebels," *New York Times,* March 20, 1993, pp. 1, 5; *Economist,* December 5, 1992.

125. Gargan, "Sri Lankan Army Makes Gains," p. 5.

126. "Tamil Separatists in Sri Lanka Offer to Talk," *New York Times* (August 19, 1993), p. A7. No time or place for such talks has been indicated, nor had there as yet been any government reaction.

127. K. M. de Silva, interview, United States Institute of Peace, Washington, D.C., April 15, 1993. In recent months the Indian navy blew up an LTTE supply boat in Indian territorial waters, killing the second in command of the LTTE.

128. Gargan, "Sri Lanka Army Makes Gains," p. 5.

129. K. M. de Silva, interview.

**130.** Early in 1993, "President Premadasa revealed . . . that military expenditure had risen from 8 billion rupees in 1990 to 24 billion, in 1992." C. R. de Silva, correspondence, January 6, 1993.

**131.** Gargan, "Sri Lanka Army Makes Gains," p. 5.

**132.** *Sri Lanka Update on Ethnic Conflict and Human Rights* (Sri Lanka Resource Centre, Oslo, Norway) 2, 8 (August 1992): 1.

**133.** C. R. de Silva, transcript, p. 56.

**134.** Ibid., p. 55.

**135.** Neelan Tiruchelvam, "Sri Lanka's Two Rebellions," *Asian Wall Street Journal*, October 7, 1991.

**136.** Ibid.

**137.** Ibid.

**138.** Coomaraswamy, "Parliamentary Democracy vs. the Presidential System: A Realist Approach," *Law and Society Trust Fortnightly Review*, August 1 and 16, 1992, pp. 1–13. Cf. Coomaraswamy, *The Sri Lankan Judiciary and Fundamental Rights: A Realist Critique* (Colombo: International Centre for Ethnic Studies), especially pp. 11ff.

**139.** Coomaraswamy, "Parliamentary Democracy," p. 8.

**140.** Ibid., p. 9.

**141.** *Report of the Presidential Commission on Youth* (Colombo: Department of Government Printing, 1990), pp. 13–14.

**142.** Ibid., p. 82.

**143.** Ibid., p. 83.

**144.** Ibid., p. 90.

**145.** Ibid., p. 41.

**146.** Ibid., p. 90.

**147.** Ibid., p. 89.

**148.** Coomaraswamy, "Parliamentary Democracy," p. 13.

**149.** Ibid.

**150.** Ibid.

# 7. Conclusion

**1.** "Although most Sinhalese are Buddhists and the majority of Tamils are Hindus, the present dispute was never religious, although journalistic shorthand in the foreign press and news agencies suggested otherwise." Barbara Crossette, "Hatreds, Human Rights, and the News: What We Ignore," *SAIS Review* 13, 1 (Winter-Spring 1993): 5. This statement stands as an unelaborated and undefended assertion.

2. See "About the Series," pp. xxvi–xxvii, above.

3. In correspondence with the author, Vernon Mendis takes explicit exception to this characterization of the situation: "My position is that while Buddhism as an aspect of Sinhala culture naturally sided with the Sinhala people it was never involved in any *jihad*-like activity to destroy or expel the Tamils in the name of a Buddhist Raj. It is the Tamils, by their terrorist attacks against Muslims and Sinhalese in the North and East, who have been guilty of a policy of ethnic cleansing from their so-called homeland." Elsewhere, Mendis continues: "The so-called militancy of Buddhism arose if at all in the nineteenth century as an aspect of revivalism, but this was true also of Hinduism. The revolt was not directed against Hindus or Tamils but against the pro-Christian colonial regime. Buddhists and Buddhism may have felt a sense of insecurity and [threat] by Tamil militancy and the demands for a separate state which militated against the historical heritage of the island. If they showed some degree of militancy it was in self-defense. To suggest that there was some kind of Buddhist-inspired *jihad* directed against Tamils because of a belief in its superiority and a notion of divine right in the island is not borne out by the facts of history."

Some of what Mendis says is consistent with the conclusions of this study. As he notes, there is no evidence that Sinhala Buddhist revivalism inspired a "*jihad*-like activity to destroy or expel the Tamils," nor is that suggested in this book. As is mentioned in the next paragraph of the text, the Sinhala tradition has been willing to suffer outsiders so long as they acknowledge that the Sinhala language, culture, and religion ought to occupy "the foremost place" in Sri Lankan society. But if there is no record of an intention to exterminate or expel non-Sinhala residents, there is substantial evidence (some of it presented in this volume) that at important points in recent Sri Lankan history, Sinhala revivalist attitudes have corresponded with discriminatory policies that have disadvantaged the Tamils, sometimes quite seriously.

Mendis seems correct, and his views are again in line with the case made in this study, regarding the development in the nineteenth century of two forms of revivalism—Sinhala and Tamil—rather than just one. Further, there is no quarrel with his claim that, in the first instance, at least, the target of Sinhala revivalism was the "pro-Christian colonial regime," rather than the Tamils. However, what appears to be missing from Mendis's account is the recognition that Sinhala Buddhist revivalism explicitly included sentiments that have to be called racist, and attitudes toward outsiders that have to be called chauvinist. Mendis is no doubt correct that at least part of the motivation behind Sinhala revivalism was a sense of insecurity in face of the perceived threat of Sri Lankan Tamils combining with and drawing strength from the huge Tamil community of South India. In that sense, Sinhala Buddhist revivalism acts out of "self-defense." However, a plea of self-defense does not excuse all. It is questionable that something so central to the revivalist agenda as the claim to cultural and religious preeminence is worthy of defense, particularly if that claim can be shown to countenance discrimination. However much Sinhala militancy is formed in reaction to Tamil initiatives, it is a central conclusion of this study that the claim to preeminence, tinted as it is with notions of racial and religious superiority, must bear considerable, though by no means total, responsibility for ethnic strife in Sri Lanka. It follows that changes will need to be made not only in the way Tamil nationalists act and think of themselves, but also in the way Sinhala nationalists act and think of themselves.

4. Tambiah, *Sri Lanka*, pp. 139–140.

# Appendix: UN Declaration against Intolerance

Resolution Adopted by the General Assembly [on the Report of the Third Committee (A/36/684)] 36/55. *Declaration on the Elimination of All Forms of Intolerance and of Discrimination Based on Religion or Belief.*

*Considering* that one of the basic principles of the Charter of the United Nations is that of the dignity and equality inherent in all human beings, and that all Member States have pledged themselves to take joint and separate action in co-operation with the Organization to promote and encourage universal respect for the observance of human rights and fundamental freedoms for all, without distinction as to race, sex, language or religion,

*Considering* that the Universal Declaration on Human Rights [General Assembly Resolution 217A (III)] and the International Covenants on Human Rights [General Assembly Resolution 2200A (XXI)] proclaim the principles of non-discrimination and equality before the law and the right to freedom of thought, conscience, religion and belief,

*Considering* that the disregard and infringement of human rights and fundamental freedoms, in particular of the right to freedom of thought, conscience, religion or whatever belief, have brought, directly or indirectly, wars and great suffering to mankind, especially where they serve as a means of foreign interference in the internal affairs of other States and amount to kindling hatred between peoples and nations,

*Considering* that religion or belief, for anyone who professes either, is one of the fundamental elements in his conception of life and that freedom of religion or belief should be fully respected and guaranteed,

*Considering* that it is essential to promote understanding, tolerance and respect in matters relating to freedom of religion and belief to ensure that the use of religion or belief for ends inconsistent with the Charter, other relevant instruments of the United Nations and the purposes and principles of the present Declaration is inadmissable,

*Convinced* that freedom of religion and belief should also contribute to the attainment of the goals of world peace, social justice and friendship among peoples and to the elimination of ideologies or practices of colonialism and racial discrimination,

*Noting with satisfaction* the adoption of several, and the coming force of some, conventions, under the aegis of the United Nations and of the specialized agencies, for the elimination of various forms of discrimination,

*Concerned* by manifestations of intolerance and by the existence of discrimination in matters of religion or belief still in evidence in some areas of the world,

*Resolved* to adopt all necessary measures for the speedy elimination of such intolerance in all its forms and manifestations and to prevent and combat discrimination on the grounds of religion of belief,

*Proclaims* this Declaration on the Elimination of All Forms of Intolerance and of Discrimination Based on Religion or Belief:

## Article 1

1. Everyone shall have the right to freedom of thought, conscience and religion. This right shall include freedom to have a religion or whatever belief of his choice, and freedom, either individually or in community with others, and in public or private, to manifest his religion or belief in worship, observance, practice and teaching.

2. No one shall be subject to coercion which would impair his freedom to have a religion or belief of his choice.

3. Freedom to manifest one's religion or beliefs may be subject only to such limitations as are prescribed by law and are necessary to protect public safety, order, health or morals or the fundamental rights and freedoms of others.

## Article 2

1. No one shall be subject to discrimination by any State, institution, group of persons or person on the grounds of religion or other beliefs.

2. For the purposes of the present Declaration, the expression "intolerance and discrimination based on religion or belief" means any distinction, exclusion, restriction or preference based on religion or belief and having as its purpose or as its effect nullification or impairment of the recognition, enjoyment or exercise of human rights and fundamental freedoms on an equal basis.

## Article 3

Discrimination between human beings on the grounds of religion or belief constitutes an affront to human dignity and a disavowal of the principles of the Charter of the United Nations, and shall be condemned as a violation of the human rights and fundamental freedoms proclaimed in the Universal Declaration on Human Rights and enunciated in detail in the International Covenants on Human Rights, and as an obstacle to friendly and peaceful relations between nations.

## Article 4

1. All States shall take effective measures to prevent and eliminate discrimination on the grounds of religion or belief in the recognition, exercise and enjoyment of human rights and fundamental freedoms in all fields of civil, economic, political, social and cultural life.

2. All States shall make all efforts to enact or rescind legislation where necessary to prohibit any such discrimination, and take all appropriate measures to combat intolerance on the grounds of religion or other beliefs in this matter.

## Article 5

1. The parents or, as the case may be, the legal guardians of the child have the right to organize the life within the family in accordance with their religion or belief and bearing in mind

the moral education in which they believe the child should be brought up.

2. Every child shall enjoy the right to have access to education in the matter of religion or belief in accordance with the wishes of his parents or legal guardians, the best interests of the child being the guiding principle.

3. The child shall be protected from any form of discrimination on the grounds of religion or belief. He shall be brought up in a spirit of understanding, tolerance, friendship among peoples, peace and universal brotherhood, respect for freedom of religion or belief of others, and in full consciousness that his energy and talents should be devoted to the service of his fellow men.

4. In the case of a child who is not under the care either of his parents or of legal guardians, due account shall be taken of their expressed wishes or of any other proof of their wishes in the matter of religion or belief, the best interests of the child being the guiding principle.

5. Practices of a religion or beliefs in which a child is brought up must not be injurious to his physical or mental health or to his full development, taking into account article 1, paragraph 3, of the present Declaration.

### Article 6

In accordance with article 1 of the present Declaration, and subject to the provisions of article 1, paragraph 3, the right to freedom of thought, conscience, religion or belief shall include, inter alia, the following freedoms:

(a) To worship or assemble in connexion with a religion or belief, and to establish and maintain places for these purposes;

(b) To establish and maintain appropriate charitable or humanitarian institutions;

(c) To make, acquire and use to an adequate extent the necessary articles and materials related to the rites or customs of a religion or belief;

(d) To write, issue and disseminate relevant publications in these areas;

(e) To teach a religion or belief in places suitable for these purposes;

(f) To solicit and receive voluntary financial and other contributions from individuals and institutions;

(g) To train, appoint, elect or designate by succession appropriate leaders called for by the requirements and standards of any religion or belief;

(h) To observe days of rest and to celebrate holidays and ceremonies in accordance with the precepts of one's religion or belief;

(i) To establish and maintain communications with individuals and communities in matters of religion and belief at the national and international levels.

### Article 7

The rights and freedoms set forth in the present Declaration shall be accorded in national legislations in such a manner that everyone shall be able to avail himself of such rights and freedoms in practice.

### Article 8

Nothing in the present Declaration shall be construed as restricting or derogating from any right defined in the Universal Declaration on Human Rights and the International Covenants on Human Rights.

*73rd plenary meeting*
*25 November 1981*

# Members of the Working Group on Religion, Ideology, and Peace

**Kevin Avruch** is a professor of anthropology at George Mason University, Fairfax, Va. He specializes in Israeli society and politics.

**Stan De Boe** is a Roman Catholic priest who is the Trinitarian Order's director of the Ministry to the Persecuted Church. He was formerly the religious liberty associate at the Institute on Religion and Democracy, Washington, D.C., where he was program coordinator for the USSR Christian Resource Center.

**Francis Deng** is a senior fellow at the Brookings Institution, Washington, D.C. A former distinguished fellow at the United States Institute of Peace, he focuses on religious and ethnic conflict in Africa.

**Lubomyr Hajda** is a professor at the Russian Research Center, Harvard University, Cambridge, Mass. His areas of specialization include the role of religion in the society and politics of Ukraine.

**Hurst Hannum** is a professor of international law at the Fletcher School of Law and Diplomacy, Tufts University, Medford, Mass. A former peace fellow at the United States Institute of Peace, he is an expert on human rights law and minority rights, subjects on which he has written extensively.

**James Turner Johnson** is university director of international programs at Rutgers University, New Brunswick, N.J. He has strong expertise in Christian theology and in religion and the control of violence.

**Mark Juergensmeyer** is a professor of sociology at the University of California at Santa Barbara. He has considerable knowledge of religious nationalism and conflict in Asia, with a particularly strong focus on religion and violence.

**John Kelsay** is an associate professor of religion at Florida State University, Tallahassee, where he teaches courses in ethics and Islamic studies. His areas of expertise include comparative religion, with a significant background in Islam.

**Samir Khalaf** is a visiting professor of sociology at Princeton University, Princeton, N.J. His areas of study include Lebanese society and politics, on which he has written several books.

**Sidney Liskofsky** is the former director of the Jacob Blaustein Institute for the Advancement of Human Rights of the American Jewish Committee, New York, N.Y. He is a specialist on international organizations and international human rights and was formerly a member of the Executive Committee of the International League for Human Rights.

**Ian Lustick** is a professor of political science at the University of Pennsylvania, Philadelphia. He is an expert on government, politics, and society in Israel.

**Sulayman Nayang** is a professor in the African Studies Department at Howard University, a department he chaired from 1986 until 1993. He has written extensively on African, Middle Eastern, and Islamic affairs.

**Gerard Powers** has been an adviser on international affairs to the United States Catholic Conference, the public policy arm of the Roman Catholic Bishops of the United States, since 1987. He is an expert on religion in Eastern Europe, the ethics of war and peace, and the conflict in Northern Ireland.

**Abdulaziz Sachedina** is a professor of religious studies at the University of Virginia, Charlottesville. He specializes in comparative religion, with a particular focus on Islam in the Middle East.

**John P. Salzberg** is director of the Working Group on the Question of a United Nations Convention on Religious Intolerance, Washington, D.C. He is a specialist in international human rights, with a strong interest in UN consideration of the issue of intolerance based on religion or belief.

**H. L. Seneviratne** is a professor of anthropology at the University of Virginia, Charlottesville. He is a specialist on religious conflict and intolerance in Sri Lanka.

**Elliot Sperling** is a professor of Central Eurasian studies (formerly Uralic-Altaic studies) at Indiana University, Bloomington. His areas of specialization include Tibetan history, Sino-Tibetan relations, and Buddhism.

**Stanley Tambiah** is a professor of anthropology at Harvard University, Cambridge, Mass. He is an expert on the history, government, politics, and society of Sri Lanka and has considerable general knowledge on the issue of ethnic conflict.

**Robert Thurman** is a professor of religion at Columbia University, New York, N.Y. He is a specialist on the role of religion in the politics and society of Tibet.

# Index

# United States Institute of Peace

The United States Institute of Peace is an independent, nonpartisan federal institution created and funded by Congress to strengthen the nation's capacity to promote the peaceful resolution of international conflict. Established in 1984, the Institute meets its congressional mandate through an array of programs, including grants, fellowships, conferences and workshops, library services, publications, and other educational activities. The Institute's Board of Directors is appointed by the President of the United States and confirmed by the Senate.